The Essential Guide to
Starting and Running
a UK Street Food
Business

The Essential Guide to
Starting and Running a UK Street Food Business

by Chris Flatt

Orders: Please contact Hospitality Active Ltd, at www.becomingachef.co.uk
You can also order via the e mail address
chrisflatt2003@yahoo.co.uk

The Essential Guide to Starting and Running a UK Street Food Business

by Chris Flatt

ISBN: 978-0-9935196-1-1

First published in 2016

Typeset for Hospitality Active Ltd by Kiryl Lysenka, Ukraine.

Printed in Great Britain for Hospitality Active Ltd by:
CMP (uk) Limited, Poole, Dorset

Contents

Introduction

Welcome to *How to Start a Street Food Business in the UK*. This guide has been designed to help you prepare for starting and running a street food business in the UK. The street food business in the UK is growing year on year with many new entrepreneurs taking up a position in the profitable street food business.

There is a lot of competition with street food entrepreneurs, and not all of the businesses will be successful. With 75% of new business failing in the first two years, this could be seen as a concerning statistic, or by a matter of choice, you can take the view that you will be one of the 25% that will be successful and expanding by the third year. With buying this guide, you have certainly taken the first step to becoming a successful street food entrepreneur.

This book has been divided into easy-to-read sections taking you through the core areas needed to prepare and run your business. This step-by-step guide needs to be read carefully, and you will, undoubtedly, come across some important information. You may have a great idea as you work your way through, so take notes as you progress. Don't ever give up on your dreams, and if you really want to start and run a successful food truck, van, trailer, or gazebo street food business, then you can do it.

To be successful, you will need to put in a lot of preparation and research; however, your hard work needs to be in-depth in the right areas and focused correctly. This will help to maximise your chances to become a successful street food entrepreneur. This guide will teach you the important core areas that you will need to focus on to be successful.

The way to start and run a street food business is to develop your own skills and experiences around the core areas that are required to be a street food entrepreneur. Many people will not focus on these areas comprehensively enough to succeed; nevertheless, it is the core areas that will create a strong foundation to build on and to become successful.

This guide will cover each area step by step. As you read through the chapters and study them, you will be able to answer critical questions that will come up, such as the following:

- Is a street food business right for me?
- How much do I need for start-up costs during the first year?
- How do I choose products to maximise profits?
- What equipment will I need and how much does it cost?
- Pros and cons of a truck (van), trailer and gazebo.
- How do I brand and name my street food business?
- What legal requirements do I need to understand?
- How do I operate safely and legally?

You will also learn skills such as how to create a menu, where to find all the equipment you will need and how to write a business plan. In addition, you will learn how to gain a competitive advantage over your competitors by successfully using the Internet and social media. There is also a chapter designated to give vital street food industry contact details.

More questions that will be answered in this guide include the following:

- What training qualifications and licenses do I need?
- What pitfalls do I need to be aware of?
- How do I hire, manage, and motivate staff?
- How do I apply to a market organiser to trade?
- Do I need an accountant?

- How to leverage free marketing?
- Why do street food businesses fail?
- Vital industry contacts with contact details.

Perhaps you want to embark on a rewarding new career or you're a budding chef entrepreneur, dreaming of having a branded street food empire. You may even be on your way to opening your own restaurant and need a starting point for your concepts. You may have recently completed a professional cookery course and are looking for a way to get your ideas out there.

If you've a passion for food and cooking, and you dream of having your own business, then starting a street food business is a fantastic choice to put forth your ideas. There's never been a better time with the street food business booming in the UK and growing year on year. I believe anyone can become a successful street food entrepreneur with the right attitude, with being prepared and with perseverance.

Thank you for your desire to learn about the business, and we wish you all the success in making your dreams come true as a street food entrepreneur.

Please – read on ...

Preface
by Christopher Flatt

I started writing this guide as a way for people who are currently working in the hospitality industry as chefs to have all the information they need to start a food business in a growing market. I believe starting and running a street food business is achievable by anyone with the right preparation and by focusing in-depth on the correct core street food business areas to become successful.

In 1997, I started my chef career at a Brasserie-style restaurant in Cambridge and have worked since that time as a successful chef for over 17 years. In the course of my career, I have worked in many establishments including hotels and restaurants, and most recently, I spent over three years at an event catering company in London learning all of the aspects of a successful catering business.

Event catering is a form of outside catering and the style of catering where all foods are prepared in a commercial kitchen and the food is then sent out to events, festivals, private dinners, barbecues and weddings, along with a team including the chef who manages the serving of the food. Presently, this area of catering offers a great opportunity to individuals who want to own their own catering business. In the UK, a fantastic trend continues to develop related to this style of catering known as the street food concept.

Street food catering, like many other forms of catering, is becoming more and more popular in the UK. Nowadays, in addition to enjoying concepts with a unique selling point, people are more aware of the foods they are eating in regard to the quality and health factors. With all this growing awareness about food, it is an ideal time for an entrepreneur to start running a street food business. Many people are taking on the challenge to start their own business.

Starting a street food business doesn't have the same costs as starting a restaurant, and it can be run on a part-time basis. For this reason, it is a more achievable business for many people. You do not need years and years of training as a professional chef to be successful. With good quality food and unique selling points, I believe anybody can become successful as a street food entrepreneur by using this guide.

Throughout my career and working life, I have always found that if I apply myself and focus on the job in hand, I will be successful. I strongly believe that with preparation and perseverance anybody can be successful in what they do.

Best Wishes...

Christopher Flatt

CHAPTER 1

So You Want to Start a Street Food Business

Within this chapter, I'll tell you about the different aspects needed to start and run a street food business in the UK. We examine the different types of outside caterers including event, mobile, festival and street food caterers and what constitutes street food. This chapter also shows you the core skills needed to start and run a street food business and the personal qualities a food entrepreneur may need. We also look into the pros and cons of working as a street food entrepreneur, the advantages of a partnership, what preparation is needed before trading starts and how much money can be made.

The Different Types of Outside Caterers

First, outside catering is a form of catering that serves mostly hot food at public or private events with the preparation of foods taking place somewhere else. There are a range of outside caterers out there working the markets, festivals, events and also as a private hire option, although there are distinct differences between the types of caterers. Here is a look at the more common types of outside caterers in business in the UK today.

EVENT CATERERS

These are caterers who are based in a unit kitchen, usually on an industrial estate. The catering operation will be full time and will work the whole year round, and is run similar to a restaurant business. They will have a range of quality menus serving functions that include weddings, canapé receptions, private dinners and so on.

MOBILE CATERERS

This style of caterer can be seen on the sides of roads, in business complexes or even car parks in their mobile units. The style of food is usually simple without a unique concept, and the foods offered are not of the best quality.

FESTIVAL CATERERS

These are large units which appear mostly at the biggest festivals and events out there. These types of units will be serving foods that can vary in quality and use a larger team of staff.

STREET FOOD CATERERS

Street food caterers are the types of units serving quality foods, which use good ingredients. They will have a unique selling point and a certain uniqueness that sets them apart from the rest.

What Is Street Food?

Street food can be described as a growing concept to serve quality food with individuality. The foods can be served from a range of places, including markets, festivals or special events. The growing trend continues with street food being one of the most innovative and interesting concepts in the UK catering scene.

Companies serving street food must use quality-sourced ingredients and serve high-quality foods. The owners will concentrate on one product and will prepare and serve this food to a high standard. Street food traders can operate and serve their products from any type of unit; for example, food can be served out of a truck (van), a trailer or a gazebo. The key point for success in this undertaking is to brand your individuality.

The Trading Places

There are broad ranges of outdoor places where a street food business can be set up to trade. You can obtain a description of the different trading places and the types of food they may serve. However, a street food operation can be set up at any of these places with the correct preparation and research. Street food is about quality and individuality, and it is usually operated by the owner with a staff if needed.

EVENTS

Catering at events is a main part of the mobile food industry. The growing demand for quality food and a broad range of choices are great for street food businesses. Customers and organisers are demanding more quality products in today's event catering.

FESTIVALS

Catering at festivals is a large operation, wherein many of the operators will have larger catering units run by a staff but managed by the owner. The owner will rarely work in the units and the food is usually mass-produced. This offers street food business owners an opportunity to establish themselves at festivals as more customers are looking for quality and a choice of foods. Catering at festivals will require an excellent organisation and a lot of hard work, but the prices for pitches (rental spaces) are high, However, the ROI can be excellent.

MARKETS

There are many opportunities around the UK for gaining a pitch on a market, which will give the caterer the opportunity for regular work. There will be markets local to your area, and most of them will offer a food that traders can pitch. These pitches can be purchased or rented on a pay as you go basis.

FUNCTION CATERING / PRIVATE HIRE

Providing a function service within a street food business is a great idea for extra work. Functions could be private events such as corporate lunches, birthday parties or weddings. The food will be prepared in a kitchen unit, with finishing touches taking place at the event where the food will be served.

Skills Needed to Run a Street Food Business

Will a street food business be the type of business that is suited to you? Do you have the skills needed or do you need extra training? There is a range of abilities that you will need to be a successful street food entrepreneur. These core skills can all be gained through training and experience; however, you should be willing to learn them if you need to, and following this guide is a fantastic first step to becoming successful.

COOKING SKILLS

You will need a basic understanding of cooking practices. You should be able to cook your selected foods well, following excellent recipes. The preparation will need to be uncomplicated, and choosing foods with a quick service is essential.

MARKETING SKILLS

Understanding and being able to market your business is essential in building your brand. Marketing will include being able to build and promote a website and to have a social media presence.

BASIC MATH SKILLS

When taking customers orders, you must be able to add the prices up quickly. This will help you as you are taking in the money and giving back the correct amount in change. One tip here is not to make the prices complicated; for example, adding up £5 + £5 + £4 = £14 is a lot easier than adding up £4.75 + £5.20 + £4.25.

BUSINESS SKILLS

You may have had experience in running a previous business and acquired important business skills there. Essential business skills will include basic knowledge on how to start a company and how to keep a healthy budget on target.

Be an action taker and know the long-term outcomes you want to achieve in your business before you start. Having a long-term goal set is highly recommended.

Personal Qualities & Attributes of a Street Food Entrepreneur

Before you start your business planning and invest time and money into your concepts, it's essential to find out if you have the personality traits to run a successful street food business. The following is a list of personal qualities that need to be under your chef's hat:

BEING SELF-MOTIVATED. Do you just want to become a street food entrepreneur, or do you really, really want it. The more you want to become a success, the easier it will be to deal with the inevitable mistakes and obstacles that will appear. There will also be a lot of hard work involved when running your business, so a burning desire to succeed must be in your heart.

A PASSION FOR FOOD. You will need to understand how to create good tasting food. This chosen entrepreneurship will require you to be passionate about creating and serving good quality foods.

5

BEING A RESPONSIBLE PERSON. To start and run your own business you will have to assume a lot of responsibility. It will be up to you to oversee your operation, so you need to be a person who is detail oriented. Also keep in mind that you will be taking on more responsibility if you need to hire help for your business, such as payroll accounts and scheduling.

GOAL ORIENTED. Having set goals to work towards and steps to follow will help you greatly in achieving your dreams. Establishing goals should be a first priority, so you know what to aim for in your business.

WILLINGNESS TO LEARN. There is a lot to learn when starting and running your own business, and there may be new areas where you have a learning curve to scale in order to acquire additional skills.

UNDERSTANDING TECHNOLOGY. There is a lot of technology that can be used in today's businesses to help any business owner move forward including making use of websites. Computer skills are a necessity in the world today and will help with the organisation of documents, the research of recipes and useful business statistics.

THINKING ON YOUR FEET. Problems will occur, and you will need to be able solve problems quickly. In-depth preparation will help prevent many problems; however, they assuredly will arise and a certain amount of improvisation will be needed.

CUSTOMER SERVICE. You will be serving the public, so a rapport will need to be built with customers. Being nice is always good for strengthening customer relationships and for building successful working relationships.

You will not need to have all of the above skills as you start your business, but they are all skills you eventually will need to develop to run a successful street food business. With patience, perseverance and hard work, it is possible to achieve your success as a street food entrepreneur.

Take An Honest Look At Yourself And See If You Are Motivated By The Right Reasons

Pros and Cons of Working as a Street Food Entrepreneur

Street food entrepreneurs come from all types of backgrounds. Owners may have had a hospitality career or recently finished a cooking course or are looking to completely make a change in career direction. Some of the best and worst aspects of the business are listed below.

Pros   **⊕ CUSTOMERS SATISFACTION**

Receiving compliments from your customers is a great feeling and energy booster. It makes all the hard work you have put into preparing and cooking well worth it.

⊕ EXPRESSING YOUR IDEAS

Owning your own street food business means you must make all the decisions on how the business is run. The business can be run exactly as you decide how you want to express yourself through your food and concepts.

⊕ BUILDING A BRAND

Starting and running your own street food business is a great way to try out your concepts and build a successful brand. A successful street food business can be the starting point for testing out your restaurant ideas if you want to move into the restaurant business later.

⊕ BEING AN ENTREPRENEUR

Running your own business is a great choice of career. You will be able to make all of your own decisions and have control over when and how you work.

⊕ IT'S POSSIBLE TO WORK FULL TIME OR PART TIME

When starting your business as a street food entrepreneur it is possible to start your business on a part-time basis. Weekends and evenings are the best times to run a street food business, so for this reason it makes a doable undertaking whilst still maintaining a regular job. A street food business can be started as a part-time job and eventually grow into a full-time job to the point where it's not possible to do both jobs.

Cons ⊖ THE HARD WORK

There is a lot of work that goes on behind the scenes of a street food business. This will include the preparation that will need to be done to get food ready, the planning of menus, the sticking to budgets and having all the licenses and permits in place, along with keeping on top of new health and safety regulations. There are many tasks that need to be taken on before a service even starts, and when it does, this can mean hours of standing and serving customers in a busy, cramped hot environment.

⊖ MAINTENANCE OF THE UNIT

The unit will need to be kept in a good working order. Trucks and vans are essential to your business and breakdowns will be a problem. If your vehicle is out of action, then you have no business and no money. Make sure the vehicle is kept in working order by having regular checkups and a backup plan should be in place for any breakdowns.

⊖ DIFFICULT TO EXPAND

A street food business is a difficult business to scale up and expand as the operation is usually owned and run by one or, maybe, two people. There will not be enough of a cash flow to expand easily. It's important to understand if you are looking to get bigger at a later date, you should have a plan in place to do so from the beginning. A well-branded business that is easy to set up and run will be less difficult to scale through a possible franchise system.

The Advantages of a Partnership

Having a partner is not essential to running a successful street food operation, and this will be your own personal decision whether or not to take one in. However, two partners who complement each other's skills and have an understanding of the other will work extremely well as a partnership. With many street food businesses being run by two people, many of these partnerships are married couples. A partnership is something to have a serious look at because by getting into a good partnership great results can be achieved.

ADVANTAGES OF A PARTNERSHIP

- **Two people will have more skills working together** – One partner could be great at customer service and the other at food concepts; this makes for a great team.

- **Expanding your business will be easier** – As you both have knowledge of your business, each could take on an operation at a different location at a later date.

- **Unpleasant jobs can be divided equally** – There will be tasks that need to done that nobody wants to do; these can be shared evenly between two people. Also sharing jobs that each individual is good at is highly recommended.

Areas to Look at When Deciding on a Business Partnership

For a good partnership to work, there are certain criteria that should be considered to gain a successful partnership. A good partnership can last a long time to great effect, however, get this wrong, and it could cause problems to your business. Areas to seriously look into include the following:

- You both need to have the same goals and ambitions for the success of your business.

- You should have similar ways of solving problems.

- Both partners need to have the same work ethic.

- Each Individual should have certain skills that work well together when combined with the other one.

Being able to work as part of a team will always work out better in the long run, since simply more can get done. However, both parties will have to want to work in a team, and if there needs to be a final decision maker, this needs to be worked out. Usually within a team, a natural leader will come through after a period of time.

How Much Money Can Be Made in a Street Food Business?

Substantial amounts of money can be made as a street food entrepreneur, although this is not a get-rich-quick method. Profits will be achieved thorough preparation, hard work and gaining valuable experience.

The amount of money you can make will all depend on how much focused work you put in. You will also need to take control of your budget and stick to a plan to keep on top of finances; reducing wastage is a critical area that will need to be worked on.

For example, if you have put some work in and gained a pitch for one day a week and earn £750 from this pitch that's what you will earn. If you have put a lot more focused work into your business and start implementing marketing methods that have been recommended further in this guide, then you could do three pitches a week, bumping up your earnings to £2250. At the moment, there exist a lot of opportunities for a street food business to make high profits.

With focused hard work in the correct core areas, you can be successful. However, remember when working out your potential profits that your costs and fees will need to be taken out of your gross receipts, but this will still leave a good amount. The highest costs areas will include pitch fees, ingredients and staff wages.

A direct effect on what problems may occur depend on the equipment you are using and the investment you have made in your business. Equipment problems will occur in all types of units; the older the unit is, the more problems that may arise. Although buying an older truck/van/trailer may create more issues with equipment than a new one, it can add character to your brand, and this may make up part of your planned unique selling point. If you are on a budget, then you may need to buy older units and equipment. Be prepared by having your equipment serviced and thoroughly checked regularly, especially before an upcoming large event.

THE UNIT / VEHICLE

The unit / vehicle is going to be the highest priced item of equipment in your street food business. There will be pros and cons to buying an older vehicle, but the initial costs are going to be lower, along with creating character and helping to brand your business. However, the older the engine is, the more work that will be needed to keep it up to standard to prevent issues, and this can be expensive and a big worry. Always make sure the MOT is kept up to date, and that it is serviced at regular intervals.

A Task List to Be Completed Before Trading

There are a number of tasks that need to be completed before you begin trading from your street food business. And it is your job to make sure all of these tasks are fully completed. A downloadable template can be found at www.becomingachef.co.uk for you to use, tweak as you wish.

The time it takes to complete the essential tasks will vary depending on your experience. However, you will find that certain tasks will take a little longer to complete when you first start going through them, and this will improve by practicing and gaining experience.

At the end of this step-by-step guide, there is a comprehensive chapter on vital industry contacts that will help you to complete certain tasks on your job list. For example, where do you complete a food hygiene certificate, and how do you get a five-star-food-hygiene rating for your street food business? I will also have the links on my website to essentials contacts for a successful street food business.

CHRIS'S TIP

Set goals to achieve each task by and stick to it; this will give you the planning and steps to keep your business starting on time.

CHAPTER 2

What Are the Start-Up Costs and Potential Profits?

Within this section, we are going to have a look at the start-up costs of a street food business and the potential for making a profit in today's outdoor catering sector. Start-up costs will vary from person to person as to how much capital the individual will have and the amount that they are willing to invest. A street food business is a great opportunity for people on a tight budget as a first business, but there are also opportunities for people with more capital to investment. We'll then follow with a look into how pitch fees are calculated and the potential profits from pitches.

The Start-Up Costs of a Street Food Business

The start-up costs to become a street food entrepreneur hinge on your finances and ability to borrow. Nevertheless, for a basic set-up, which serves a simple style of food, you will be looking at a range starting at £4000 to £5000; this will include the pitch fees. You will then need to take into account additional costs on top of that, such as a truck/van or trailer. It is also possible to rent trailers and trucks from one day upwards. There are also franchises available for street food businesses, if you are looking for a ready-made model to start and run.

There are a lot of costs to consider when you are preparing to start your street food business; here is a guide to what type of set-up will be available to various budgets. I have included a costs sheet for the prices of important documents you will need and the basic equipment. There are industry contact details further on in this guide for equipment and important information.

Options for Three Levels of Investment

The start-up costs for starting a new brick and mortar business are high in hospitality and catering. A mobile street food business gives a lot more people the opportunity to take on a food business at a far lower cost. You need to estimate what your budget will be able to achieve. The finances you will have available to invest will need to be worked out, and a suitable business started in an appropriate catering area within your budget.

BELOW £5000

This budget is the starting point and will fund a business in the purchase of a second-hand trailer in full working condition for small events and roadside catering. You will be able to set up a stall in a market and have all the basic equipment. A hog roasting / baked potato business set-up will be within this range.

£5000–£10000

At this medium price range, more opportunities start to open up. You will be looking at financing a new small to medium-sized trailer or a used trailer that is in very good condition with opportunities available at shows, fairs, events, markets or festivals. Within this range, used food trucks and vans will become affordable and also more pitches will be within your means.

£10000–£20000

At this price range, a higher quality business set-up can be achieved. You could be looking at a new mid-range to a much larger trailer working at shows, fairs, events, markets and festivals. Good quality truck and van conversions are within this range and a higher amount of quality event / festival pitches can be attained.

£20000–£40000

This next price range level will mean new, larger, high-quality trailers and vans can be part of the business set-up. Catering at events and festivals with a higher range of pitch prices will be possible.

£40000 AND UPWARDS

A new custom-styled large van / trailer conversion catering for the biggest festivals in the UK will make your business part of an elite group.

The equipment each business will need varies on the food that will be served and the unit that is being used. Below is a list of equipment that may be used, including the essential 'survival kit' that every set-up should have.

THE MAIN UNIT

Franchise	£10000+
Pop-Up / Gazebo	£69.99+
Truck / Van	£8000+
Trailer	£1000+
Leased / Hired	1 day hire = £450 1 week hire = £550

BASIC ESSENTIALS

Napkins	× 200	£3
Cups + Lids	× 50	£7
Chopping Boards		£15
Basic Utensils + Knives	Selection	£30
Plastic Containers	× 5	£5
Cooler Box	× 1	£35
Fold-Up Prep Table	× 1	£45
Hand Wash Unit	× 1	£100 – used
Menu Display	× 1	£10
Water Container + Tap	× 20 litre	£15
Rubbish Bin	× 2	£10

COOKING EQUIPMENT AND SAFETY

Gas Cooking Grill	× 1	£350
Gas Bottles and Extras	× 1	£90 First, Refills are cheaper
Fire Blanket	× 1	£15
Fire Extinguishers	Each	£20

CERTIFICATES

Food Hygiene Certificate	Each	£15
Public Liability Ins.		£120–£160
Gas Safety Checks	× 1 Check	£35
PAT Certificate	Minimal Fee	£75

THE SURVIVAL KIT

Cleaning Products	Selection	£50
Food Probe	× 1 + Wipes	£10
Paper Towel	× 1 Blue Roll	£1 Each
Catering First Aid Kit	× 1	£20
Kitchen Wear	Cloths + Aprons	£20
Bin bags x 2 types	× 1 Roll Each	£5 Each
Clingfilm – Small	× 1	£4 Each
Tin Foil – Small	× 1	£4 Each
Salt and Pepper	× 1 Each	£2 Each
Small Chopping Board and Knife	× 1 Each	£5 Total Cost

These prices are a guide and are a starting point for basic ready-to-use quality equipment.

A Guide to Pitch Fees

Some locations you want to trade at will have a set pitch fee to pay, and then you can trade your products. Other events and festivals require you to offer a tender, which is the amount of money you think the pitch is worth. You offer the tender and the organiser will decide on which caterers to use at the event.

RESEARCHING THE PITCH FEE FOR A SUCCESSFUL OUTCOME

The first thing that needs to be understood is that there are several parties who are looking to make money out of the event / festival. The organiser will want a high return from traders, and the traders will want to maximise their profits. Profits need to be fair for both parties, and a good working relationship needs to be built. You as a trader need to come to a sum that you are willing to pay after doing your research on the event and sticking to it.

HOW TO RESEARCH AN EVENT

You need to understand the facts about the event to ensure your success. The fee you will offer and pay (also known as the tender) needs to be calculated, so it is fair. You will need to gather all the important information you can about the event to be prepared to succeed. There are three main areas that need to be researched.

What Are the Attendance Figures Expected?

The event organiser will give a maximum number of people that can be attracted to the event, so a good method is to halve the numbers they give you. In most cases, previous attendance figures can be obtained from the local licensing office to give a more accurate estimate.

What Is the Competition and What Are They Selling?

The amount of other food traders will affect your profit for example. An event expecting an attendance of 4000 attendees with 10 food traders means a share of 400 customers each. An event expecting 4000 attendees that has only 5 food traders will create an 800 customer share. This projection needs to be taken into consideration when calculating a fair pitch fee.

How Many Attendees Will Buy Food?

The type of event needs to be looked at and examined. For example, do the attendees have alternative places to eat outside the arena? At a three-day music festival, attendees will be in one place with no alternatives other than what is on offer at the event. What foods will be suited to the event type, and how often will people eat? Look at the demographics of the crowd for spending habits, because professionals with disposable incomes will spend a lot more than teenagers with little disposable income at an event.

MAKING A PROFIT

Working as a street food entrepreneur, you have to make a good profit; if there is no profit in an event, you should walk away from it.

AN ESTIMATE OF FOOD SPENDING HABITS AT EVENTS / FESTIVALS
These figures are a guideline only and your figures may vary.

- Music Festivals 70%–80%

- One-Day Shows 50%

- Local Markets 40%–55%

You do not want to take a risky gamble with your finances, so you should only offer and pay for a pitch what you can afford. A simple calculation to work out your tender, based on the estimated food spending habits table.

Firstly make a realistic decision on how much portions of food you can deliver in one day, for example 300 portions. Your portion set a price of £5 will calculate at 300 × £5 = £1500. Your tender needs to be calculated from this sum at between: 10%–25% therefore you would offer between: £150–£375 for the pitch rent. Don't be afraid to negotiate the fee if you feel the organiser's fee is too high, you may also be able to pay a percentage of profits only instead of a set fee with some organisers when negotiated well.

YOUR PITCH
Check the location of your pitch on a site map that you are tendering for. Being in the middle of the arena where all the attendees will be ready for food and being around the back are very different. Make sure the location is good if not don't be afraid to walk away you don't want to pay for the worst pitch at an event.

GET A WRITTEN CONTRACT AGREEMENT
Make sure you have a contract made up around what the organiser has agreed. If the organiser has verbally agreed that there will only be 8 traders at an event get this in formal writing. If you arrive at the event and there are 20 traders you will have evidence to use and can sue for loss of earnings. If a contract in writing has been refused, then this will be extremely concerning.

SOME EXAMPLES OF PITCH FEES TENDERED

3 Day Music Festivals £10000 per pitch

3 day Events £500–£750 per pitch

1 Day Markets £60–£100 per pitch

The Potential Profits

These are the investment levels available for a full working street food business depending on the investment level, know we need to look at the potential gross profits available in a street food business. I have a section further in this guide that will go into gross profit in more detail. Below is a calculation of what gross profit percentage needs to be targeted and also a look at cost and selling prices to achieve profitable gross profits. There is also a gross profit calculator contact at the end of this guide that will instantly calculate your gross profit.

POTENTIAL GROSS PROFIT LEVELS

Gross profits within a street food business can be very high compared to other businesses. An average gross profit margin will be between: 65%–85%. With a reasonable achievable goal set at a 75% target. However, street food businesses have been able to reach a 90% gross profit level.

Put simply, if you are targeting to achieve a certain profit, follow these guidelines:

- **A 70% gross profit** you will need to sell £1 of ingredients for £3.33.

- **A 80% gross profit** will be £1 of ingredients for £5.

- **A 90% gross profit** will need £1 of ingredients being sold for £10.

A quick and basic calculation to use to arrive at a selling price using a set gross profit target is quite simple: (Cost of ingredient) × 4.

Example,

Cost = (£1.50) × 4 = £6 – A £6; selling price will be a 75% Gross Profit Margin.

Any odd numbers in the final price can be rounded up to make the service faster.

NET PROFIT CALCULATION

To achieve a net profit all the other expenses will need to be subtracted including the new equipment, wages and pitch fees. If you have a good business model and do not waste a lot, then a very good profit can be made.

Understanding what a gross profit is and how to achieve it is an essential core concept to learn and develop. I have mentioned gross profit several times within this guide, as it is an essential part to starting and running a successful street food business. Get this wrong and it needs correcting immediately.

CHAPTER 3

What Type of Street Food Business to Run?

In this section of this guide, we will be looking at the different types of units there are to choose from, including the types of foods to build your food concept around. I have also included a table of popular main ingredients and their cost, so you can get an idea of your outlay for foods, their portion costs and a possible selling price at a gross profit of 75ЖЮ This is going to be probably the most daunting part of starting your street food business. We'll then follow with a look at the different ways of working with popular UK street food and additional income streams that can be added to a street food business.

The Different Types of Business Set-Ups – The Unit

A TRUCK / VAN – THE PROS AND CONS

The most popular choice for street food caterers is the truck/van. This unit is the most mobile and will come in a range of sizes and levels of quality. This type of unit will have a kitchen built into the back of it. They can be purchased ready-made or it is possible to have a truck/van custom built, which can range in size from 16–30+ feet in length, and the kitchen will be fully functional. As with all commercial kitchens, they will need to follow all relevant health and safety laws with regular inspections and have all required licenses. Licenses, rules and regulations will be covered further on in this guide.

The food trucks and vans' biggest advantage is their mobility. It's far easier to travel to and from events than with other type of units, and it's possible to do several small events on the same day. They can be parked easily at events and for storage. The kitchens are a good size and can compete with the trailers in kitchen space.

If you have an older vehicle that fits your concept, then breakdowns can occur as with any older vehicle. The vehicle will need to be serviced at regular intervals, and it's recommended to have a full roadside breakdown cover for emergencies. However, investing in a good vehicle from the start will save a lot on repairs, and you will have the peace of mind that your vehicle will not regularly have problems.

A TRAILER – THE PROS AND CONS

The catering trailer is a trailer with a fully fitted inside kitchen following all health and safety regulations. The trailer is a lot more reliable as it usually has fewer problems that can occur, but you will need a dependable vehicle to tow the trailer and the relevant sections of your driving licence need to be completed. However, if you do not feel comfortable with towing a trailer, this may not be a good choice of unit. Unlike a truck/van the catering trailer is going to need to be towed by another vehicle as it is a lot less mobile.

The trailer can be branded easier than a truck/van; branding wrap will need to be added to the outside by a professional. The trailers have more space inside them than a truck or van, so a busy service will be more comfortable to work through.

A GAZEBO – THE PROS AND CONS

The gazebo set-up is the most affordable type of selling platform to use; a gazebo can be yours for £70> However, if you are looking at setting up a quality street food business from a gazebo, it is recommended to use a superior branded gazebo. You will be able to buy a quality gazebo and a custom designed gazebo from around £180 and upwards. Gazebos can be set up in many places that a truck/van or trailer will not be able to get to, and the space is well laid out for a gazebo set-up With a gazebo set-up, you will be working outside, so you may need to wear a fleece due to outdoor temperatures in the colder months.

CATERING HUTS

These units are what you usually see at many Christmas festivals and German-style markets. The unit will be flat packed and built up on site. There is a lot of work that needs to be done to put this type of unit together and to take them down. These types of units are suitable for longer events, such as festivals lasting from a few weeks to a month and for Christmas markets.

UNIQUE VEHICLES FOR CUSTOM BUILT UNITS

Mainly food trucks / vans are built from the standard trucks and vans; other vehicles that can be converted into a street food business include busses, ambulances and fire engines, which can create a unique concept and design.

Choosing a Concept and Food Style

Choosing the concept of your street food business is very important. When choosing your food for your street food business, there are a number of important factors to take into consideration including what consumers actually want and how you will give that to the consumers. Also, the preparation and cooking times of foods will need to be understood.

The decision on your food will have a knock-on effect to the rest of your business – from menu items to the branding of your unit to the speed of your service. Other considerations to make are to estimate how much gross profit will be made and to choose the right recipes that you or a new staff member can easily follow, which should not be complicated.

For example, some concepts out there include the following:

- A Fire Engine Unit Serving Fiery Hot Dogs

- A Van Designed as a Bowling Green Serving Meaty Balls

- A Trailer Designed to Look Like a Burger Serving Burgers – The Tasty Burger

Some popular foods that can be served from a street food business are identified in the list below:

Example Types of Popular UK Street Foods to Help Design a Concept

Burgers	Breakfast
Toasted Sandwiches	Thai
Barbecue	Health foods
Pulled Pork	Falafel and pitas
Hot dogs	Vegetarian / vegan
Tacos	Panini
Mexican	Mac and cheese
Pizza	Basil Chicken
Organic	Chicken wings
Mediterranean	Stews
Soup	Fish and chips
Italian	Bakery
French fries / chips	Nuts
Korean	Pancakes
Popcorn	Vegetable / fruit juice

Working with Popular UK Street Food

Street food ideas can take inspiration from all over the world. When choosing your style, think about what customers you are targeting; for example, a trendy street food market in London will have different food needs than a countryside county show.

When deciding on your food, take into consideration the preparation times, cooking times, cost of ingredients and serving speed needed. It is recommended to have as much preparation work done as possible the day before your event. The better your preparation for an event, the smoother and faster your service will be. A range of different foods will take longer to prepare than a limited menu and the service speed can also vary considerably.

A NOTE ON HOT HOLDING

Hot holding is a way of holding foods at a safe temperature following the health and safety regulations. This method is most suited for foods that hold heat well including stews, soups and sauces. A burger will not be suited for hot holding, as it will become very dry. All hot holding needs to be done safely and with foods that are not going to lose their quality.

BURGERS

A very popular street food item is the burger. Burgers can be made in advance; however, the cooking times for burgers are longer, so it's good to have a few ready and to cook more as you start to run down on them. The ingredient costs are low if using a beef mince, but the preparation time will be longer for homemade burgers.

STEWS (BEEF STEW FOR EXAMPLE)

A traditional beef stew will have a longer cooking time, but the service of the food will be very quick. The service will just need a spoon for the stew to be put onto a disposable serving dish whilst the stew will be hot holding in a bain-marie. You could offer extras such as a mini puff pastry lid premade or a spoon of mash that can also be made beforehand and would be hot holding. The ingredients for a stew will be less expensive as a cheaper cut of meat is used for the preparation. However, a stew will need about a three-hour cooking time when cooking in large quantities.

INDIAN FOOD (A CHICKEN KORMA EXAMPLE)

Indian food is very popular in the UK with a broad range of foods. For example, the chicken korma curry can be made the day before and reheated on the next day and placed in hot holding in a bain-marie. A chicken curry has a long cooking time in order for all the spices to cook into the sauce, but will have a good profit margin as a diced chicken thigh can be used and is a cheaper cut of meat. Rice can be cooked on the day and have hot holding in a bain-marie.

BANGERS (SAUSAGES)

Be unique and use the best ingredients to offer a quality dish. There are many sausage street food entrepreneurs out there, so being able to offer a unique concept can be difficult. Organisers of these events are looking for variations in what the food traders will be serving.

BREADED FISH AND CHIPS / POTATO WEDGES

Breaded fish and chips are an alternative to battered fish and chips. The fish can be breaded the day before and cooked in the fryer on the event day. Chips can be blanched the day before, which means it will be half cooked and finished on the actual day. This will create a medium service time as the fish will take 4 to 5 minutes to cook; a good tip here is to keep the size of the fish thin, so it cooks quickly. The cost of the ingredients can vary – a lower cost fish can be used such as coley, or a higher end concept could use a fish such as plaice. Chips / potato wedges can be made using a good potato variety. This will work in a truck / van kitchen set-up, as there will be a high usage of equipment including fryers, fridge and hot-holding equipment.

PASTA

Pasta needs to be done well, which means making the sauces fresh and using high-quality ready-made pasta or freshly made pasta. A street food concept needs to be based around quality ingredients that are cooked well and are flavoursome. The ingredient costs can be kept down, so a great gross profit can be made although the service can be slow. Essentially, the pasta will need to be drained properly after reheating and overcooked pasta is not very nice. Sauces will need to use in-season ingredients to produce the best results. It's far better to keep the dishes simple with a twist and use in-season ingredients with a first-class recipe.

ROLLS, BUNS, PANINIS, GRILLED SANDWICHES & SAVOURY CREPES
There are a wide variety of hot sandwiches, buns and crepes that can be developed for a menu. A key point is to always have a hot filling for a product; for example, a spiced pulled pork food can be added to a roll or bun easily, or hot-grilled sandwiches are popular options, such as toasties and paninis.

DESSERTS
Dessert street food operations are a good idea, as they will complement the savoury options open to the customers. Crepes are a very popular dessert to have at an event; however, it needs to be a unique idea. Other British favourite desserts to consider: sticky toffee pudding and sticky toffee sauce, apple crumble and custard, or a bread and butter pudding. These types of desserts all have a low cost to produce and can be made in advance, and then reheated and held for a service.

ADDITIONAL INCOME STREAMS
Beverages including tea and coffee can be simply added to most food concepts and are a high profit margin product.

Food ideas need to be kept under control. This means that you can have a unique concept, but not to be too far out there so that people are confused as to what you are producing. Simple food done uniquely in season and freshly made is the direction to aim for as a street food entrepreneur. So, give the customers what they want.

It's recommended to allow on the menu around 10Ж for vegetarian options of the foods you are serving. If you are serving burgers, you could have veggie burgers ready to serve, or if you are serving a curry, have a vegetarian curry option available. The trick is to keep the vegetarian options related to your main food to keep preparation and serving times down.

A Guide to the Main Ingredient's Cost

AND THE SELLING PRICE TO ACHIEVE A GOOD GROSS PROFIT TARGET SET AT 75%

Main Ingredient	Portions	Total Cost	1 Portion Cost	Selling Price @ 75% GP
@ 75% GP	25	£35	£1.40	£5.60 + Extras
Chick Thigh × 5kg	30	£30	£1.00	£4.00 + Extras
Stewing Meat × 5kg	30	£34	£1.13	£4.50 + Extras
Pork Shoulder × 5kg	18	£30	£1.66	£6.70 + Extras
Coley × 2kg	16	£18	£1.12	£4.50 + Extras
Plaice × 6 Fillets	20	£30	£1.50	£6.00 + Extras
Rice × 1kg	20	£4.75	£0.23	£1.00 + Extras
Pasta × 1kg	10	£3.10	£0.31	£1.24 + Extras
Potatoes × 1kg	8	£1.50	£0.18	£0.75 + Extras

All prices and portion controls are an average cost to be used as an example only. These are all from my own working experience. It's recommended to test your portion sizes to gain an accurate gross profit margin.

When working out your selling price, all of the ingredients (+ the extras) will need to be added together at the gross profit margin that you want to achieve. Wastage will affect your final profit and needs to be kept under control. It is easiest to have a recipe made for your dishes, and then you can work out the cost of ingredients to consistently achieve your gross profit (GP).

KEY POINTS WHEN DESIGNING YOUR BUSINESS CONCEPTS INCLUDE THE FOLLOWING:

The Unit Type

- Truck/van, trailer or gazebo.
- Theatre of the operation – and is music from your unit allowed?
- Think about your pitch placement – are you next to a similar stall?

The Food

- What do people want?

- How do I give it to them?

- Choosing what to sell.

- Do one thing and do it very well.

- Ingredients cost – preparation and service speeds.

- Profit margins from different dishes.

- Health and safety friendly.

- Make up a dish that excites you – if it excites you, it will excite customers.

CHAPTER 4

Keep Continuously Improving Your Business

In this section, we look at the importance of continuously improving and developing your street food business. Areas covered include 'How to find out who your customers are' and 'How to drive your sales'. We also look into 'How to research your competitors' and 'How to compete with them'. A SWOT analysis can be essential to your continued success and we take a look into the important SWOT analysis. Then we look at an example of a market research test questionnaire that can be used and tweaked as you wish.

Continuously Improving Your Business

Once your street food business is ready to go and you have started trading, you will need to spend time working on your business development. There are many areas to concentrate on, and you should always be looking for ways to improve your product. This could be an improved recipe or better quality ingredients. Perhaps, you could cut down on your wastage or further develop brand awareness. A very important area to pay attention to and continuously improve on is your customer service, because a happy customer who has had a good experience will promote your brand by recommending you to others by word of mouth or by social media. A customer with a bad experience can be extremely bad for your business, especially in today's world of instant social media. This could result in bad reviews on social media sites or other review sites like TripAdvisor where you need good reviews. Having a happy customer is fantastic and compliments are tremendous to receive making all the hard work meaningful. However, always treat negative customers politely. Listen to their complaints, take them on board and try to rectify the complaint as best you can. Smile, communicate well, be patient with your customers and maintain a polite tone.

Who Are Your Customers?

There are many different categories of events to work at all over the UK, and your customer will vary with the location and the type of event. When you have a clear product and developed brand, you will be able to identify your ideal customer and where to find them. There are important considerations to weigh when identifying your ideal customer: the sex – male or female; the specific age range of your ideal customer as a festival with 18–20 years old will have different food expectations than a show where the age range will be 65+: and where do your ideal customers live and how much disposable income do they have?

Know your customers and what they want and can afford.

Once you understand your ideal customer, you will be able to target these customers and what they are looking for before they make a purchase.

Example of Two Types of Customer at Events

A 2-DAY CURRENT MUSIC EVENT
Average Customer Age: 18–30
Disposable income: Medium
Children: No

A 2-DAY MOTORHOME SHOW
Average Customer Age: 40–70
Disposable income: High
Children: Yes

From the two examples above, it's possible to see how a street food concept can be developed to target specific customer types. The two examples can be targeted by two different concepts in food and in branding. Additional revenue streams can be made by focusing on whether or not children will be present. It's highly unlikely to have children at a popular music festival and highly likely at a motorhome show due to parents bringing their children. Therefore, having a children's option can be profitable too.

UNDERSTANDING HOW TO DRIVE YOUR SALES
Your street food concept can be promoted in a number of ways that will include your website, social media profiles and how you are presenting your unit. Listing your features and benefits is a key area to promoting your street food concept. This is how to identify your features and benefits; first, what are a feature and a benefit? A simple way of looking at this is how will the feature benefit the customer.

Feature – a specific quality or attribute of your business, as your feature will provide a benefit to the customer. You will need to identify the specific features of your concept; these could include the following:

1. Child-friendly items on the menu.

2. Vegetarian option on the menu.

3. A very quick service.

4. A 5-Star Food Safety Rating.

Benefit – the benefits of your business are the specifics that will motivate your target customers to buy your food. What the customer will achieve by buying your product:

1. Customer finds food their children will like.

2. A vegetarian customer will find suitable food they will like.

3. A customer in a rush will get served quickly.

4. Customer is confident of your good food quality and practices.

All of your features can be turned into benefits. Going through this system will help you to find your strongest benefits. By practicing this method, you will be able to identify your strongest benefits and be able to use them in your preparation to market your business and attract your target customers to buy from you. Customers will be able to understand your brand and meaning, and with this will come trust and higher sales.

How to Research Your Competitors and Compete with Them

FIRST – HOW TO IDENTIFY YOUR COMPETITORS

Your job at this point in your preparation is to identify who your competitors are. When you have identified them, it will be possible to research them and develop a better product. Competitors can be identified in two categories: your direct and indirect competition. The direct competition will be the street food businesses serving similar foods as your business, and the indirect will be the businesses operating in your selling price range at the same events and festivals as you are. Indirect competitors will offer a different style of food, but will attract a percentage of the customers. Once the main competitors have been identified, you need to research them.

NEXT STEP – HOW TO RESEARCH YOUR COMPETITORS

As we go through our strategic plan, the next step will be to find our competitor's best and worst activities. By doing so, we will be able to make a plan to get ahead of them in the street food marketplace. This is known as gaining a competitive advantage.

Important Strategic Information Needed

- Identify my top three street food business competitors.
- What range of foods do they sell?
- Are my top three competitors making money?
- Is the business growing or reducing in size?
- How long have they been operating?
- What benefits do they give the customer?
- What negative aspects do they have in a customer's opinion?
- How have they priced their products?
- How do I make my business unique from my competition?
- What are their daily customer numbers?
- What is their competitive advantage (if any)?

Keep all of your research data from your competitors. And start building a records file that can be analysed to compare and assess your top three street food competition businesses. Once we know the questions to ask to get the information we are looking for, we will need to gather as much as we can.

FINALLY – HOW TO GATHER IMPORTANT INFORMATION ON YOUR COMPETITION

Now your job will be to gather important research information, and this can be done in a few ways. Visit your competitors at an event or festival as a customer, order some food and ask questions of the operators about their street food business. Get a good understanding of their customer service and compare it to your own.

Social media is a good place to search for interesting facts, deals, events and festivals being attended by your competitors. Social media profiles include those on Facebook, Twitter and Instagram, where you can like their profiles and then receive their news that will show up in your news feed. A lot of good and bad points can be found on review sites such as TripAdvisor.

Fully research your competitors' websites as this may describe any awards they have won or show magazine/newspaper articles regarding them, and read their blogs, which also could have a lot of information about them and what they do. Researching your competition on Google is a great source of information, not just their website but also any other web pages that may be valuable sources of information.

The SWOT Evaluation in a Street Food Business

A SWOT analysis is a structured system to plan the four different areas of a business – **strengths, weaknesses, opportunities and threats**. The SWOT analysis for your street food set-up should specify the objectives of the business. It will allow you to identify the internal and external aspects of your business that hold positive and negative factors that you will need to deal with in order to reach your goals.

STRENGTHS

The strengths of your street food business will include all the things you are better at than anybody else and what makes your set-up better than the others. Any strength that you have needs to be used as a base for future business decisions. An example could be that you are a highly experienced chef.

WEAKNESSES

The weaknesses of your street food business will include the areas you can improve upon to help move the product and service forward. Understanding the weaknesses you have will make them easier to work around. An example could be that you have a small amount of funds.

OPPORTUNITIES

Opportunities are essential to identify for the continued success of your street food business's development; to find those opportunities, we evaluate our strengths and weaknesses. An example could be that, as an experienced chef, you can create some inspirational new dishes using cheaper cuts of meat and other ingredients.

THREATS

It is essential to identify the threats to our street food business, such as any potential issues that could occur. Potential issues may include the cost of ingredients going up or a street food business similar to ours entering the same events or festivals and offering food items at lower prices.

Remember that when you are using the SWOT analysis, you will be asking and answering questions that will develop important information about each SWOT category. This information is critical to find your street food business's competitive advantage.

An Example of a SWOT Analysis for a Street Food Business

STRENGTHS

1. A highly trained and experienced professional chef.

2. Good established relationships with food suppliers to get best prices.

3. A better quality product at similar prices to our competitors.

WEAKNESSES

1. Limited direct customer service experience.

2. A limited amount of money to invest in our business.

3. No experience in large events such as a 3-day music festival.

4. Child-friendly menu options are currently unavailable.

OPPORTUNITIES

1.   High-quality street food is a growing trend in the UK.

2.   Partnering with a local business to start up a cookery school.

3.   Adding a wedding and corporate function option to our business.

THREATS

1.   A direct competitor lowering their prices.

2.   A new relevant health and safety regulation being introduced.

3.   Our trading unit being damaged or vandalised.

Well done! This is a big step to pinpoint each component because identifying your strengths, weaknesses, opportunities and threats are crucial in your business planning. If your objective that you put in place at the start of your planning has become unreachable, then an alternative option/goal can now replace it. Once your new goal has been set, then a repeat SWOT can be done to make sure your new goals are now attainable.

How to Use This Important SWOT Analysis Information

The next step is to use the important SWOT information that has been gathered and researched to attract the highest number of customers to your street food business.

The strengths of your street food business that have been identified need to be understood, so that you can concentrate on giving your customers what they want. For example, one strength of your business could be the ability to produce great foods because you are a highly experienced chef. In this case, your food is satisfying the customers, so you can then focus your attention on improving your customer service.

However, events can turn in a different direction. According to the SWOT analysis, the business is serving great food due to the owner being a skilled chef who turns out a superior product to the main competitors. What happens if your competitor hires a chef to develop some outstanding recipes at a lower price? To retain your competitive advantage, you will need to come up with new and inspiring ideas using the chef's skills and reducing the cost of the ingredients.

If a weakness that has been identified is keeping potential customers away, then we can improve it. For example, if we do not have child options on our menu, are we keeping customers with children away from our business – that is quite possible? So, by adding child options to the menu, we put in place a foundation for a wider customer base. This could just mean making a smaller portion of a menu item. If we have a quality spicy burger for sale, we could add a smaller burger with no spice as a child's option.

We have identified the possible threat of a unit being damaged or vandalised whilst being parked when not in use; in this case, we can locate a safe vehicle storage area. Discovering your vehicle has been damaged before an event or festival due to it not being securely parked can result in a large amount of money being lost.

CHRIS'S TIP

A SWOT analysis needs to be taken at regular intervals to keep your competitive advantage.

Testing a market to find out what they want is essential to having a successful business. I have developed a testing questionnaire that may be used as a tester on markets. The questionnaire can be tweaked and used as you feel it is necessary, and this type of test can be used on Facebook lists or groups for example.

The Market Research Test Questionnaire

1. What do you understand about street food?

2. Is street food an option you would consider eating?

3. Do you like *(food concept here)* food?

4. Would this be a lunch or dinner style food for you?

5. What do you understand about this type of food?

6. Do your children like this type of food?

CHAPTER 5

Writing a Business Plan

In this chapter, we will look into the details of creating a business plan, as no guide on starting a successful street food business would be complete without the ALL-IMPORTANT business plan. A detailed plan will help you to map out your business idea, assess its viability and form an action plan for your new business in its early days.

The Business Plan

The best business plans will explain only the most essential information. They'll list what you want to achieve, how you intend to get there and what you will need to do along the way.

Below I have included a sample template for a business plan. The contents and notes are what would normally be expected in a plan, but should be altered to suit your own requirements. Before completing the document, you will need to have done some research into competitor activity, pricing and the market for your services/products etc.

Business Plan Template

(Insert the name of your business here), Date (month and year)

SECTION 1 – MANAGEMENT SUMMARY

This is a summary of the plan and is better left till all the other information is filled out.

SECTION 2 – BACKGROUND OF THE BUSINESS OWNER(S)

- Give a short personal and business background, showing areas that are relevant to your proposed street food business, including skills and experience that will be used in the business.

- Include things that you need to learn, to ensure that you can run your business well. How will you learn these new skills? When do you plan to learn them?

- Why do you want to run your own business?

- Previous work experience;

- Qualifications and education;

- What knowledge/experience do you have of the food industry and what training have you completed?

- Details of future training courses you want to complete;
- Consider a SWOT analysis as described previously in this guide.
- Any additional information.

SECTION 3 – PRODUCT OR SERVICE OFFERED

- Give a detailed description of your business or service (not too technical);
- Use bullet points;
- Include pictures if relevant.

SECTION 4 – YOUR CUSTOMER/TARGET MARKET

- Who are your target customers?
- How many are there? Why should anyone want to buy what you provide? What is your evidence for this and what market research has been carried out? Are there enough customers for your business to be viable?
- **Describe your typical customer in detail;**
- Where are your customers based?
- **What prompts or motivates your customers to buy your product / service?**
- Market Research – provide evidence and detailed findings of your market research. Give facts rather than 'your interpretation'. Be objective. You could use any of the following to help with your research:
- Questionnaires – provide a copy of any used;
- Test trading;
- Word of mouth;
- Internet / Trade Contacts / Surveys;
- **Is there a demand for your service or product?**
- How big is the market/demand?

- Current trends up or down – detail how you found this out;

- Any important facts and statistics on whether the market is seasonal or dependent on other external factors, like the weather;

- Your own knowledge or past work experience.

- What factors help your customers to choose which business to buy from?

- Have you sold products/services to customers already?

SECTION 5 – COMPETITION

- Who are your competitors and how many are there?

- Direct Competitors – those selling the same or similar products/services.

- Indirect Competitors – those selling alternative products / services.

- Why should anyone want to buy from you and not from your competitors?

- What is your USP (Unique Selling Point) – why are you different?

- What will your customers look for when buying from you or your competitors?

SECTION 6 – MARKETING AND PROMOTION

- What information/facts are you going to tell potential customers about your product/service to encourage them to buy from you?

- What are the features of what you sell?

- What is the benefit to your customers?

- What methods are you going to use to reach your potential customers?

- Why did you select these methods and how will you measure the success or failure of your marketing?

- What offers and promotions are you going to use under each of the following categories:
  - Attracting new customers;
  - Building loyalty / retaining customers;
  - Encouraging each customer to spend more.

SECTION 7 – PRICING AND COSTING

- How have you arrived at your selling price?
- What is the cost to you of producing this product/service?
- What are your competitors charging?

SECTION 8 – SALES FORECAST

- What value of sales do you expect to make each month in the first year?
- It is unlikely that your sales will be the same in every month of the year, so show your monthly sales estimates.
- Show how you have calculated these and explain (in words) how you have arrived at the monthly values. For example, have you considered seasonality and other reasons why customers might spend more or less money with you in different months?
- Give a summary of how confident you are of achieving the forecasted sales.

SECTION 9 – ADMIN & LEGAL REQUIREMENTS

- What paperwork do you need to put in place before you start trading: terms and conditions, insurance, licenses, quote forms, invoices, receipts etc.?
- How are you going to keep control of all your business information, on the computer or manually?
- What information are you going to collect? For example, customer details, employee details, and stock and financial information.

- How will you keep your financial records? What legal aspects do you need to consider?
  - Health & Safety
  - Food Hygiene/Safety
  - Local Council permission
  - Required types of insurance
  - Public Liability
  - Employers' Liability
  - Stock/business asset cover

SECTION 10 - START-UP COSTS

- List all costs incurred at start-up, including equipment already purchased for use in the business, explain how you will fund this.
- Also include how much money you are planning to borrow (if any).
- Costs of starting your set-up may include:
  - Premises
  - Equipment
  - Transport
  - Materials/Stock
  - Upfront payments
  - Marketing

Loan Required = £

Your Personal Survival Budget
You will need to calculate how much money you are going to need to survive whilst starting your business. This may include the following:

- Monthly cost (£)
- Mortgage/rent

- Council tax
- Gas, electricity
- Water rates
- All personal and property insurances
- Clothing
- Food and housekeeping
- Telephone
- Hire charges (TV, Sky etc.)
- Subscriptions (clubs, magazines etc.)
- Entertainment (meals and drinks)
- Car tax, insurance, service maintenance, personal car running costs
- Credit card, loan and other personal debt repayments
- Family/partner, part-time job
- **Total income (£)**

Total survival income required (£)

CHAPTER 6

Marketing and Social Media

In this chapter, I'll give you some crucial explanations of how to get started on the Internet. In today's street food business market, it is essential to get ahead of your competitors. The best way to do this is to use the Internet as a marketing tool. We'll be looking into how to set up a website and the importance of social media. I'll give essential information on Facebook, Twitter and Youtube. Then we'll go through how to build a social media campaign with my Social Media Presence Builder.

Using the Internet as Part of Your Street Food Business and Brand

There are many different ways of using the Internet to your advantage when marketing your operation. If used correctly, the Internet is a cost-effective business tool, and it provides a great way of reaching thousands of potential customers.

Here are just a few ideas of how the Internet can be used to your advantage.

By using the Internet, you are can obtain up-to-date events, festivals and more that are not readily available elsewhere. Businesses within the street food industry can gain immensely by finding out about the latest trends and by responding to them before their competitors do. With the introduction of pay-per-click advertising, new street food set-ups can advertise their product or their services straightaway. There is a broad range of opportunities to advertise on the Internet, for example, Google AdWords and Facebook ads. The great benefit of this type of advertising is that your ads can target specific customers. This can be used to great success within a business.

More and more street food businesses are using the Internet as a place to advertise and promote themselves. The great thing about the Internet is that it is very fast, easy to use and more and more people are using it every year.

I strongly believe that EVERY new street food business needs to have some form of online presence. When starting your street food business, you may have a tight budget to stick to, and you should seriously consider setting up your online presence by yourself.

The Internet is filled with different and sometimes confusing terminology.

Here are a few terms to help you come to grips with basic definitions:

URL

The URL of a web page includes everything that appears in the address log of your browser, such as http:// and everything that comes after it when you visit a web page. URL is short for 'Uniform Resource Locator', or simply 'website address'.

DOMAIN NAME

The part of a website address that identifies the site as belonging to a particular domain, and can be used to locate organisations or other entities using the web.

BLOG OR WEB LOG

A blog serves as a form of personal journal for any individual on the Internet. These can either be public or private.

BROWSE

Browsing refers to the act of exploring or searching for useful links and pages on the Internet.

BROWSERS

Browsers are software programs that enable you to view the world wide web (www) pages, for example, Chrome or Firefox.

CACHE

In browsers, the 'cache' refers to the space where your Internet viewing history is recorded.

COOKIE

This is a message that is sent from a web server computer to your browser. The information sent is then stored within the browser. When your computer interacts with the original server, the cookie will be sent back to the server, allowing it to respond according to what was in the original cookie.

FTP

File Transfer Protocol (FTP) refers to the ability to transfer entire files from one computer to another, whilst keeping them intact for usage.

HOST

This is a computer that provides web documents to clients or users.

HTML

Hypertext Mark-up Language (HTML) is a language based in computer code, which is used for all web-based formatting, including textual content, images and applications. Whenever you look at a web page, you are looking at the final product of endless reams of HTML code, working in conjunction with your browser.

IP ADDRESS OR IP NUMBER

An Internet protocol (IP) address or number is a unique number, consisting of four parts separated by dots, for example – 149.116.245.2. Every machine that is on the Internet has a unique IP address. Most machines also have one or more domain names, which are far easier for people to remember.

Purchasing a Web Domain Name

The first step to getting started on the Internet is to purchase and register a domain name. It is important that your domain name is unique, as Internet users will access your website using this. For example, a domain name for a quality burger street food business called the Tasty Burger could be www.tastyburger.co.uk and this is what the domain name looks like. Your domain name should be relevant to your business as this will help with your branding. The most popular domain in use is '.com' and is called a top-level one; it can even be found in the common English dictionary. Other examples of domain names that you can purchase are as follows:

.co.uk – commercial/general
.gov.uk – government (central and local)
.ltd.uk – limited companies
.mod.uk – Ministry of Defence and HM Forces public sites
.net.uk – ISPs and network companies
.nhs.uk – National Health Service institutions
.plc.uk – public limited companies
.sch.uk – schools (primary and secondary education)

The domain name for your business is totally up to you. An important thing to remember is that your domain name needs to be catchy and easy to recall. An example would be 'becomingachef', which is easy to recollect and says what it does. Try to come up with a good name for your website.

The next step to take, once deciding on your domain name, is to check to see if it is available for purchase. The Internet has been operating for many years, so the name you are looking to register may have already been taken, as a result you may need to slightly change your choice. It's possible to contact the owner of a domain you want that has already been registered. However, it is advisable to register a domain name that is available at a small price when first starting out. Most of the .co.uk domain names can be registered for around £1.99 per year.

There are many different web-hosting sites where you can search for and register a domain name. Here is a list of some of the more common web-hosting sites:

www.oneandone.co.uk
www.domainmonster.co.uk
www.reg-123.co.uk
www.webfusion.co.uk
www.ehost.com

It is simple to check for a domain name, just enter your choice for a domain name in the search bar on any hosting site, and it will tell you if it is available or not.

Hosting Your Website

Web-hosting clients upload their websites to a shared (or dedicated) web server, which is then looked after by their Internet service provider to ensure a fast and stable Internet connection. A lot of the domain registering companies will offer web hosting in exchange for a small payment.

Building a Website

Only you can decide if your street food business warrants a website or not. When you are making your decision, you should take into consideration that more and more people are using the Internet each year. Internet traffic is growing on a daily basis, which means the potential is there to gain more and more customers to your website. Whether you plan to sell products on your site or not, it is still advisable to have your own website. A website is a good place to keep customers up to date about all of your services and products. Your contact details will be easily available on the site for customers, and you can keep people up to date about your products and services through a weekly or monthly newsletter.

Deciding how to create your website is a difficult decision. You may decide to do it yourself, and a number of web-hosting companies out there will offer a complete web creation package such as www. ehost.com. Although if you do not have experience in such systems, it can be extremely frustrating to learn how to build a website.

It is advisable to get a website built by a professional if you have no experience, and this does not mean you have to spend thousands of pounds.

There are a broad range of self-building website services out there, including www.MoonFruit.com, www.Wix.com, www.GoDaddy.com, and www.FatCow.com. Another option, if you do not want to build your website yourself, consider posting a job on www.upwork.com. This site is full of talented professionals, who can create your website at a fair and affordable rate.

PAYING SOMEBODY ELSE TO BUILD YOUR SITE

There are literally hundreds of companies out there who will create your website for you and the costs will vary. If you are selling products on your website, it is a good idea to have a professional build your site.

Before you spend any of your money, make sure you pay them a visit first and ask them questions about the service they can provide you. Whilst they may be the web design specialists, you are the only person who knows what you want.

The following are a range of important questions that you might wish to ask a web designer before you agree to a contract:

- What timescale will my website be completed within and will there be a contract to back this up?
- Are there any 'hidden costs' that I need to take into consideration?
- How qualified is the web designer?
- Will he/she keep me updated of any progress?
- What is the turnaround time and cost for any future alterations?

When hiring an outsourcer from an outsourcing website to build your website, it is highly recommended to create an example website in a power point presentation form, explaining the style and functions you want on your website. It's advisable to spoon feed the outsourcer, so that they know exactly how you want your website designed.

Advertising Using the Internet

Once your website has been set up, you will need to direct traffic to it. You will always want to attract as many Internet surfers as possible to sell your services and products. As a street food business, you could be advertising your extra services such as catering for weddings or corporate functions. Don't expect people to find your website just because you have one – the fact is you will need to advertise, and there are a number of ways to do this.

THE SEARCH ENGINES

The most popular search engines used in the UK include Google, Yahoo, and Ask, with Google accounting for over 70% of all searches. A search engine does what its name implies and makes possible searches on the Internet. The users of the site enter in a word or phrase, and the search engine provides them with a number of choices on a web page; some of the results are via natural listings and the rest are from sponsored links.

NATURAL SEARCH LISTINGS

Natural search listings appear on a web page according to the logarithmic scales of the search engines, which do not charge for the service. In most search engines, these are the 'main' results out of the hundreds of thousands or millions of possibilities listed on the Internet.

SEARCH ENGINE OPTIMISATION

Search Engine Optimisation (SEO) refers to the process of increasing visitors to your website, via increasing your website ranking in the listings of search engines such as Google. In simple terms, the higher your website is ranked in the search listings, the better the chances of people viewing the site. Similarly to web developers, there are a huge number of talented SEO specialists out there, who can be hired at a cost.

Here is a useful set of websites and services that offer SEO services:

Ayima	www.Ayima.com
Conversion Factory	www.conversionfactory.com
Conversion Rate Experts	www.conversion-rate-experts.com
Keyphraseology	www.keyphraseology.com
Page Zero Media	www.pagezero.com
Search Engine College	www.searchenginecollege.com
SEOinhouse.com	www.seoinhouse.com
Stephan Spencer	www.stephanspencer.com

There are many companies out there who will offer cost-effective 'link building' services for your website. Be very careful about employing a company or individual who offers this type of service, unless you are 100% certain they are genuine and reputable as things can certainly go wrong. You can easily get penalised by Google for having poor backlinks directed to your website, and sometimes you can even get banned! To learn more about SEO and link building, visit www.MOZ.com.

SPONSORED PAID FOR LINKS

Sponsored paid for links are a form of advertising on search engines including Google, Yahoo or MSN. These ads appear at the very top right-hand side of search engine results and are paid for. Each search engine has its own criteria of how high up the listing will appear on the web page. The performance of your advert all depends on how much you are willing to pay when someone clicks on the advert.

With pay-per-click advertising, you can design your own personal ads and choose the keywords. The keywords are phrases that connect to your business. When somebody searches for the keywords related to your business, your ad might appear next to the results in the search engines. A great advantage to this method is that your advert can be tailored to an audience that has a specific interest in your business.

A great advantage of this method is that you can now advertise to an audience that already has an interest in your services. The ad will simply be clicked to find out more about you and, hopefully, people will decide to buy from you. The difficult part in this method is getting customers to purchase when they arrive on your web site.

The majority of quality search traffic will come through Google, and it's advisable for your efforts to be focused on Google as opposed to Yahoo or other smaller search engines.

SPONSORED LINKS, TIPS AND ADVICE

Relevance is a very important when creating an ad as your keywords have to be relevant to your business services. For example, if your street food business wants to attract customers to its wedding catering service, your advert needs to have the keywords related to 'wedding catering service'. If one of your keywords is 'snow machine', the traffic from your ads will include people interested in that item, which is totally unrelated to your services. A good method used by pay-per-click advertisers is to match the advert with the keywords you are bidding on. This has more of a chance to generate a higher click through rate to your website and services.

TEST THE MARKET

If you decide to advertise your services using the search engines, make sure you test your advert first. It's advisable to create an advert relevant to your business with the specific keywords. Bid a small amount for the keywords to start with and see if you get any clicks to your website. If you do not get any clicks to your website, then you can change your ad and keywords until you find a good combination that works. As soon as you create an advert that gets click-throughs and conversions, you can pay more for your advertising as you know it's working.

A big mistake people make is to pay a lot for an advert that they have not tested because they are only looking to get their advert at the top of the results. If the advert is not converting, then this is a waste of money. When an advert starts getting click-throughs and customers are buying your services, then you can up the advertising budget.

Using Social Media as a Free Marketing Tool

Social media is a fantastic way to leverage free advertising for your street food business. Social media buttons can be added to any web page, and your web page can be linked to from your social media profiles. The key to remember here is to keep your profiles up to date by posting at least once a week. It is important to set up a presence on social media to build your brand recognition value and even sell from the site directly.

FACEBOOK

Setting up a basic Facebook profile can be done with an email address, and an audience can be built easily. Facebook is continuously developing and becoming a great business tool, which can be used by any street food business to great effect. You can add pictures and videos of your food and much more about your business to your profile. You can become a fan of other people, add friends, join groups and connect with many businesses relevant to the street food industry.

TWITTER

Another popular social media site within the food industry is Twitter, where an account can be set up easily with an email address. You can post tweets, which are limited to 140 characters, and search for other street food businesses by using #streetfood.

BLOG POSTS

Blog posts are informative and conversational posts on your website that are recommended to be 600–900 words in length. Well-written, engaging blog posts will attract people to your website and create links to other pages on your website.

YOUTUBE

YouTube is a useful way of attracting free traffic to your website and advertising your street food brand, and your YouTube channel can be set up easily with a Gmail account. You can add a video trailer to your business and as many videos as you like for free to advertise your food business. All you need is a mobile phone that has a video camera and a YouTube app to produce quality videos – a tip is to keep your videos interesting and engaging. A good length for a video will be no more than one minute for a YouTube trailer, and for a more informational video between one and two minutes in length.

INSTAGRAM

Instagram is a mobile photo-sharing platform for sharing your pictures and videos. With Instagram it is easy to share your quality content with other social media sites including Facebook and Twitter.

Example Social Media Presence Builder

MONDAY – FRIDAY

1. Add a new person or business to your list on each of your social media profiles, and share and like one of their posts.

2. Share a post of one of the profiles you are already following.

3. Share one of your blog posts each day.

4. Research a relevant topic and write a new blog post 600–900 words.

5. Make a short video about your blog post; embed this to your blog post and upload to YouTube.

Take a break on Saturday and Sunday. Following this plan will build a social media presence in about 3–6 months.

When writing your blog post, you will need to write between 600–900 words of good quality content. Research your topic on a Monday and start writing your content. It's advisable to break down the writing of the blog post, so you do a little each day taking about an hour, by doing this, you will soon have quality content on your blog and also content for your YouTube channel.

Your social media can be set up to automatically share with your other sites. So, when you add a blog post to your website, it will automatically be shared with your other social media profiles, and also by adding a post to Facebook, it will share with all of them.

Social media is a very important part of any new and established business. The more you practice with social media, the higher your quality of content will become. As mentioned previously in this guide (outsourcing sites), you could place an advert on an outsourcing site for a company to be your social media manager at a reasonable price.

For more free basic advice on setting up a social media profile, visit my YouTube channel that can be found at www.becomingachef.co.uk.

CHAPTER 7

Understanding Business Structure

The information contained in this chapter will provide you with essential tips and advice on how to set up your own business as a sole trader or a limited company. And it will give you some helpful hints on how to run your own street food business on how to start up a street food business. To follow I have given a start up checklist to be completed and Finally, I've added contact details further on in this guide, which you might find useful.

As a street food entrepreneur, there are three main ways you could decide to register as a business. The first is as a sole trader, the second is as a limited company and the third option is registering as a partnership. There are three types of partnerships to choose from: limited liability partnership (LLP), sleeping or dormant partners, and general partnership. A sole trader and a limited company are the main types for a street food business.

A Sole Trader

The simplest way to start a street food business is to register as a sole trader. This means that you as the sole owner operate the business, and you will run the business on your own. A big benefit of this approach is that you will take home all of the profits and will be free from any registration fees. A weakness is that you will need to be a very responsible person and keep on top of all the accounts. The best way of doing this is by using an accountant who specialises in the field.

You will be responsible for all of the debts that the business incurs, which can make sole trading fairly risky. However, it can be extremely lucrative if you get it spot on.

To register as a sole trader you just need to download and fill in a CWF1 form from the HMRC website. As soon as this is done and sent off, you are officially registered and can begin trading as a business.

Limited Company

Limited companies exist as individual companies, and can be registered through Companies House. The finances of a limited company are consequently separate from the personal finances of the owners. Shareholders will not be responsible for any debts acquired by the company, but could stand to lose out on their original investment if the business runs into trouble.

REGISTERING A LIMITED COMPANY

There are two types of limited companies: Private Limited and Public Limited.

Between these two types of companies, there exist a few differences. Public limited companies are legally allowed to raise funds by selling shares of their company on the stock market, but private limited companies cannot. Public limited companies must also have a share capital of £50,000 or more, with two shareholders, two directors and a trained/qualified secretary.

LIMITATIONS

Private limited companies are limited by shares, which the shareholders own. By doing so, shareholders who have paid the full amount for their share of the company cannot be held responsible for any debts acquired by the business. In spite of this, if a shareholder has not fully paid for their share of the business, they will still be held responsible for the amount that they owe for the shares. An agreement can also be put in place to regulate public limited companies. When this happens, the individuals in the partnership agree on a set liability limit.

In order to register a private or public limited company, you should visit the Companies House website at: www.companieshouse.gov. uk.

More jobs to do when registering your street food business as a company:

- Clearly display the company name on the outside of all trading units.

- The company name should be clear on all letters, invoices, receipts and cheques.

- All business letters and order-forms need to show your company's registered office address.

- All the required registration forms need to be fully completed and sent to the registrar of companies.

SETTING UP A LIMITED COMPANY:
REGISTRATION DOCUMENTS AND FORMS

To register a limited company within the UK, you must send a number of completed forms to Companies House. If your business is being set up in Northern Ireland, then your registration needs to be with the Northern Irish Companies Registry. The documentation you will need to complete and register is as follows:

- **A Memorandum of Association.** This will provide all the details about the company including the name, location and its services.

- **Articles of Association.** An important document that will describe how the company will be operated and the powers the directors will have.

- **Form 10 (Statement of the First Directors, Secretary and Registered Office).** This statement will detail the director's addresses and specific details of the company's registered office.

- **Form 12 (Declaration of Compliance with the Requirements of the Companies Act).** A document that declares the company has met all legal requests for its incorporation.

How to Set Up a Street Food Business

When setting up your own street food business, you will need to contact your local food standards agency. The agency will help you to register your business.

CONTACT YOUR LOCAL AUTHORITY

You will need to get into contact with your local authority before opening. They will help you to do the following:

- Registration of your food business.
- How to plan your business.

Learn the appropriate training needed and the equipment required. You can find the contact details of your nearest local authority at www.food.gov.uk.

REGISTRATION OF YOUR BUSINESS

Your business will need to be registered with your local authority and the environmental health service. The registration process is free, but needs to be completed at least 28 days before opening.

A start-up checklist:

....

- Are your premises registered?

- Are legal requirements met?

- Learn the main general food law.

- You must keep written records of the suppliers that provide you with food or any ingredients.

- Put safety management procedures in place and keep all records up to date.

- Keep staff training up to date in order to ensure good food hygiene.

- Have you registered as self-employed?

- Records need to be kept of all business income and expenses.

- Records need to be kept of your employees pay.

- Do you know how to pay your employees tax and national insurance contributions?

- Food and drink needs to be described accurately.

- Do you require licenses for the selling of alcohol?

- Do you require licenses for entertainment? For music?

- Do you require a license for selling food late at night or selling on the street?

CHAPTER 8

Financial Management

In this section of the guide, we will take a look into the financial management of your business. You will learn why financial management is important and how to put a system into place to ensure your business starts off on the correct path. We'll also look into how to set up a business bank account, what to do as your business grows and how to decide if you need an accountant. Finally I have given my Top 10 Tips for financial management.

Financial Management

Organising your business finances is essential when you are starting your street food business. Achieving the success you want will take preparation and hard work. You will need to organise your finances from the start or you could be setting yourself up for failure further down the line. It will definitely have an adverse effect on your success if you have poor or no financial management. The way in which you handle your finances will be critical to the success of your business. If you fail to keep on top of your bookkeeping, then the sustainability and success of your business venture will be compromised. On the other hand, keeping the business bookwork up to date will help your business in the down periods and allow you to grow it. Keeping your accounts up to date will be one of the most off-putting parts about looking after the company.

FIRST STEPS

I recommend that before you start trading, you get in contact with the local offices of the Inland Revenue and the HM Revenue and Customs. Either call them or make an appointment to see them. You can find a number of useful helplines on the Government's advisory website, using the following contact numbers:

Business Link Helpline	0300 456 3565 Monday to Friday, 9 a.m. to 6 p.m.
Business Wales Helpline	0300 060 3000 Monday to Friday, 8.30 a.m. to 5.30 p.m.
Business Gateway (Scotland)	0845 609 6611 Monday to Friday, 8 a.m. to 6 p.m.
Invest Northern Ireland	0800 181 4422 Monday to Friday, 8 a.m. to 5 p.m.

When you make contact with the relevant section, explain the details of your business plan and ask them what you need to do. You will be provided with all the essential advice that you will need to start your business correctly. Through this process, you will be given leaflets and any forms that will need to be completed, including a

VAT registration form that you may need to complete before trading. It also helps to have a contact within the local offices that you can call whenever you run into any difficulties.

BUSINESS BANK ACCOUNT

A business bank account is needed to run a successful business; this account will be the heart of your finances and will record every single business transaction. The account will be used for payments to suppliers and staff, to make withdrawals and for other transactions that are integral to running a business. A business bank account will be extremely useful for working out taxes, and can provide you with access to vital support and advice. Before setting up a business bank account have a shop around at the different deals, products and services on offer.

Business bank accounts are very similar to a standard personal bank account, although there are some extra features. A business bank account may offer these services: a company credit and debit card, overdraft and loan facilities, asset finance, factoring and invoice discounting (borrowing short term against the value of unpaid invoices) and commercial mortgage and merchant services. Merchant services will allow you to accept credit and debit card payments. To qualify for merchant services, it is often needed to have two years of trading history and audited accounts.

DO I NEED AN ACCOUNTANT?

An accountant will be a business advisor to you when you first start running your own business. They will be able to give you advice on your business plan and the tax issues of registering a new business. Some accountants offer bookkeeping services, but if they don't or if you wish to handle this yourself, you can get help with setting up manual or computerized bookkeeping systems. Most importantly, you need an accountant to assist on things such as registering for VAT or PAYE, and the procedures involved.

An accountant will also give you financial advice and help with budgeting, cash flow and credit control, along with up-to-date information on any general or legal enquiries.

AS YOUR BUSINESS GROWS

When you are starting your business, an accountant can be a great source of advice, in such areas as how to gain extra finance without risking your business. An accountant is not only managing your money but also putting controls in place to help with the growth of your business in the correct way. You may have a lot of concerns such as finance, working capital and good stock control. An accountant with experience is a source of valuable information and advice, as well as having the ability to keep your finances up to date with all the current tax issues.

VALUE ADDED TAX (VAT)

When first starting your street food business, you may not have the turnover that warrants registering your business for VAT. However, as you become more successful and start growing, you may need to register.

When you have turned over £82000 or more in the previous 12 months, you are viable for VAT. This figure is known as the VAT threshold, and it can change usually once a year, so it's good to keep an eye on your turnover compared with the current threshold.

You will be expected to account for every penny you have spent on your business; consequently, you will need to show for each month a profit/loss and income expenditures in detail, so the tax can be clearly calculated. It's possible to use accountancy software or a freelance bookkeeper that will be using the accountancy software to calculate your tax for a monthly fee.

The Top 10 Financial Tips and Advice

FINANCIAL MANAGEMENT TIP 1:
Talk to the local offices of the Inland Revenue and the HM Revenue and Customs. Either call them or book an appointment. If possible, do this before you start to trade, as this will save a lot of complications at a later date.

FINANCIAL MANAGEMENT TIP 2:
Get yourself a business bank account. Look around at what's on offer, and use all of the facilities the bank has to offer you – you can never get too much advice.

FINANCIAL MANAGEMENT TIP 3:
Right from the start, keep records of payments and sales etc. Keep all your receipts, as failing to do this can cause problems for your business accounts in the future.

FINANCIAL MANAGEMENT TIP 4:
Get yourself an accountant and book an appointment to see them. They will give you advice and information on all of your business accounting matters.

FINANCIAL MANAGEMENT TIP 5:
Hire a freelance bookkeeper, who will keep your accounts in order on a monthly basis. This will save you time, and free you up to drive your business forward.

FINANCIAL MANAGEMENT TIP 6:
Keep up to date with financial business matters, from VAT to corporation tax. Although your accountant will know all of this information, it is beneficial for you to know it too, so that you can plan and budget your finances in order to develop your business.

FINANCIAL MANAGEMENT TIP 7:
Know your business. Know how much profit percentage you make and how much you turnover. Again, this will enable you to move your business forward, or budget where needed.

FINANCIAL MANAGEMENT TIP 8:

Keep paperwork. Keep all paperwork that is relevant to the financial side of your business, even if you think it is not needed. It is better to have some irrelevant paperwork than to be missing important records, which your accountant or bookkeeper will be chasing you for.

FINANCIAL MANAGEMENT TIP 9:

Make sure you put money aside each month to cover any future VAT bill or corporation tax bill. This will prevent you from receiving any large tax bills that have not been accounted for.

FINANCIAL MANAGEMENT TIP 10:

Although the financial side of the business is extremely important, do not spend hours and hours on it. The most important elements of your business are your entrepreneurial skills and working to develop your company to achieve bigger and better things.

PROFIT AND LOSS ACCOUNTS

It is the law in the UK for companies to produce financial statements every year. These important documents will be in the form of company reports. The most important statement is the profit and loss report; the second is the balance sheet.

The profit and loss account will show how much profit or loss the business is making. This can happen in several ways, but as a street food trader, we will give an example of trading. The top section of this account is known as the trading account. The gross profit can be calculated by deducting cost of sales from the turnover.

For example: the profit and loss from a Tasty-Burger unit
Turnover: £1000
Cost of sales: £250 – therefore, the gross profit is £750 = 75% GP

Turnover can also be known as sales revenue and is calculated by multiplying the individual items sold by their average price.

For example: if the average price of your three types of burger at Tasty Burger Ltd is £6.50 and the number of burgers sold is 154, then the turnover is 154 x £6.50 = £1000

Cost of sales is all the costs added together in order to trade the Tasty Burgers. So, the average cost for 1 burger is £1.62, and we sold 154 burgers

Cost of sales is therefore: £1.62 x 154 = £250

Gross profit is then calculated by subtracting cost of sales from turnover.

Gross profit is therefore: £1000 − £250 = £250

There are also other costs to deduct including pitch fees, equipment and so on; these are known as the overhead costs or expenses. To work out the net profit, the expenses are subtracted from the gross profit.

Net Profit = Turnover − Gross profit − Expenses

THE BALANCE SHEET

The balance sheet shows an overall summary of the position of the business financially. To grow and expand your business, you will need to use your assets (what the business owns) or any monies that the business is owed. There are two main ways to finance getting assets: first, internally through capital raised by the owners or shareholders, or secondly, externally from loans etc.

Want to learn how to start a street food business?

Visit:

www.streetfoodbusinesscourse.com

Learn how to start and run a street food business through my 1-Day intensive training courses.

CHAPTER 9

Where to Trade and Presenting Your Street Food Business

In this chapter, we will be looking at the many different types of events that it is possible to be trading at. Street food is on an upward trend and, over recent years, more and more opportunities are becoming available with the trend continuing upwards. It's very important to consider your branding carefully, and here are some considerations to make when presenting your street food business at events. Followed by top 10 tips and advice when looking for event pitches and for Private Hire Catering.

Presenting Your Street Food Business

Your street food business needs to be able to attract customers; a great brand will take your business's concepts and match a look and atmosphere to it. For your branding, you will need to have a logo and a design for your unit, vans and trailers, which can be wrapped, whilst a gazebo may be custom designed. A wrap for a vehicle is a method of adding your design and logo to the unit. Creating that first impression of your business is critical to attracting customers. Vehicles can also be painted at a lower cost by a professional designer.

How to Brand a Unit

A LOGO

Your street food logo needs to be relevant to your business and eye-catching to the public. Your truck/van or trailer will be on display at an event and also as you are travelling to and from events. Two things to consider when you are creating a logo: (1) keep it simple and use a maximum of three colours, and (2) your logo needs to be adaptable for your social media profiles and your website, as your online presence and branding is essential. Once your logo has been finalised you can use it on your social media, uniforms, flyers, stickers and your website.

COPY WRITING

This is the writing on your truck, banners or boards, which needs to be kept simple and easy to read. On the unit, it should include your company and contact details. The text needs to be large enough so it can be seen from a distance.

YOUR FOOD

Any images you use of your food need to be colourful and bright, so they look good to eat and draw customers in.

OTHER AREAS

Some good examples of truck design are the supermarket home delivery vans on the roads, including Tesco and Sainsbury's trucks.

You can get some ideas from researching your competition at events and how they present themselves. Are they visually appealing, if so, how can you gain some ideas from how they present their businesses? Many events and festivals will run well into the night, so be aware that you will need lighting that will display your unit well and you can still look bright and appealing. Your menu needs to be readable and your business should always look inviting and ready to trade.

Your business should include these considerations:

- Look clean and work tidy.
- Wash your hands regularly.
- People enjoy the visual element of food and cooking – add some theatre.
- Be nice and friendly to customers.
- Wear a branded uniform; this could just be a branded t-shirt and apron.
- Get some flyers printed and hand them out – self-promotion works.

UNIT DESIGN

When you have your unit design plans ready, you will need to take the next step, which is adding your design to your unit. There are two main ways of doing this: the first is by adding a unit wrap, and the second is by painting the unit. Wrapping a vehicle is very popular with established businesses and comes at a higher cost but can last for many years.

If deciding on a wrap or painting, then employing a professional is advisable, although you can do it yourself at a more reasonable cost. I have listed quality graphic designers for vehicle wrapping further in this guide; it's a simple step-by-step process to get your vehicle branded.

Trading Locations Within the UK

The main types of trading locations for a street food business are roadsides / offices / business parks / public events / private events.

Roadsides, Offices & Business Parks

Usually this will be a business located on a permanent pitch serving foods daily. To get a profitable pitch, you will need to be in a busy area with lots of footfall or office workers, and all licenses will need to be obtained from the local council.

Events Open to the Public

There is a broad range of events open to the public throughout the whole of the UK, which offer great opportunities to a new street food business. A public event is an event where anybody can attend, and mostly they are free to the public to attend.

Public events can range from a local Sunday farmers market with hundreds of attendees all the way up to a three-day air-show festival with tens of thousands of attendees.

MARKETS

In the UK, the range of markets can be put into two categories. The first being the type of markets that are open daily, usually in town centres. The other is the specialty markets, such as the street food markets and privately run ones, which have limited trading times. Both of these options offer good rates for a new street food business to set up at, and include council markets, farmers markets, street food markets and car boot sales.

Within the UK, the trend in having open air markets is on the up-swing with the growth in street food being a contributing factor. Many food entrepreneurs are being attracted to street food as a good business venture because of the lower operating costs. Consumers are becoming more aware of their products and quality of ingredients, along with the fact that they are a leisurely way to shop.

All this is contributing to an atmosphere of relaxation and fun, much more so than shopping at the local supermarkets.

COUNCIL MARKETS & FARMERS MARKETS

These types of markets operate in a more traditional style based on a waiting list system. Many of these markets will have stalls and pitches that have been handed down in a family or occupied by traders who had been on waiting lists for many years. When your name comes to the top of the list, then you will be offered a pitch with no real interest in what you sell.

How to Get a Pitch

Contact the local council and arrange a meeting with the person who organises the market; this can be done over the phone or in person. To obtain a pitch and get onto a waiting list, you will need to contact the organiser directly; details can often be found on the local council website. Usually gaining a pitch on a farmers market will operate in the same way if it's city or town centre based. Details you will need to find out include the time frame for upcoming pitches, the pitch prices and if your street food business will be permitted on the market.

PRIVATE MARKETS INCLUDING STREET FOOD MARKETS

These types of markets are a lot more interested in the quality of food you will be selling and how your concept will fit in with the overall concept of the market. These quality street food businesses will have a variety of options for the attendees that will be available, and your brand presentation is of more importance at these events. Street food markets are usually run by private entrepreneurs and will have a vibrant trendy atmosphere with bars that may offer a range of live music. Privately run street food markets can run all day and late into the night.

How to Get a Pitch

The key here to gaining a pitch is your USP – Unique Selling Point – and that the food you are serving will complement the other food traders' offerings. With a USP that fits in well along with a great brand, there is often space available for a pitch, creating a big opportunity for your street food business.

WORKING AT SHOWS, EVENTS & FESTIVALS

There are many opportunities for a street food business all over the UK. A broad range of public events and festivals take place every year, and the majority of them will need street food traders to offer foods to attendees. The following list shows the many types of shows, events and festivals available for pitches.

- Air shows
- Farmers markets
- Fireworks displays
- Flower shows
- Food / music festivals
- Street food events
- Agricultural shows
- Trade shows

- Historical events
- Motor shows
- Pet shows
- Sports events
- Steam rallies
- Wedding shows
- Charity events
- County shows

With the broad range of events all over the UK, there are plenty of opportunities for pitches to fit your budget, experience or goals, and to create a profitable venture with the proper business foundation in place.

MUSIC FESTIVALS

The big music festivals give street food traders the opportunity to make a lot of money and a lot of profit. Being fully prepared for these big events is key to being successful. Correct budgeting needs to be worked out so all costs are covered, and a healthy profit is made. Fully planning your logistics is critical to your success. Nevertheless, if you want be successful at these events, you can be. It is to your benefit to gain as much advice as possible and plan for all eventualities. There are also smaller music festivals throughout the UK that are better suited for a new street food business.

POINTS TO REMEMBER ABOUT MUSIC FESTIVALS

- Your preparation is key to a successful operation.
- Offer a quality product from a quality unique unit.
- Adapt your product to suit a 3-day event where no extra supplies are available.
- Be prepared to be on the site the entire time to maximise opening times.
- Be aware of the food service times in your units trading area.
- Prepare your logistics in fine detail.

Chris's 10 Top Tips and Advice When Looking for Event Pitches

1. Research the organiser to make sure they are a reputable organiser.
2. If the event is new, do extra in-depth research about the company.
3. Do the event details seem to be too good?
4. Is the venue aware of the upcoming event advertised, and do their figures match what the organiser has quoted?
5. Make sure the event has a relevant license.
6. Research the company using Companies House.
7. Get a contract for the specific terms the organiser has given you.
8. If they will not offer a paper contract, red flags should be apparent.
9. Do they ask for fees well before the event date – another red flag.
10. Check the distance and travelling times.

Before you commit to paying and confirming a booking, carry out your in-depth research on events you are interested in, especially, if they are new.

Private Hire of Your Street Food Business

This is a fantastic way to run your street food business; you can focus solely on private event hiring or use it to add an extra element to your current street food operation. Private hire means your operation can be hired privately by a customer for a private event, such as weddings, corporate catering, BBQs, funerals, birthdays, or themed parties. Private hire events will mean that the customer will come to you mainly through your website. This is where an optimised website will be a great advantage over your competitors.

In a previous chapter, I explained about using online ads, which can be very useful in attracting clients. Being at the top of a Google page for a keyword search, such as 'wedding caterers Kent', will get search traffic to your site for people searching this specific keyword.

PROS

The pros of running a private hire street food operation are many. You will get paid upfront, and you will know exactly how many portions to prepare. You will also be fully prepared for your food portions, which prevents wastage, and there will be no need to handle any money.

CONS

You will also need to consider the downsides to privately hired catering for your street food operation. You need to figure out how much you will charge for an event to guarantee that you will get the job and are not underbid by another operator, whilst still making a worthwhile profit. Another concern is in how you will transport the food safely?

You may be taking jobs at places where the equipment is very limited or the space is very compact, so a certain amount of initiative may be needed to set up and serve. As with most new set-ups, it will take some time for your business to gain a good reputation. Great feedback and positive reviews will help grow your business, but you need to do the work first before you start getting good feedback.

CHRIS'S TIP

Chris's 10 Top Tips and Advice for Private Hire Catering

1. Agree on the payment terms; it's advisable to be paid in advance.
2. Agree on how many portions you will serve beforehand.
3. Make a serving time plan; however, be flexible to this on the day.
4. Be aware of any dietary requirements.
5. Agree on children's portions beforehand.
6. Ask if they want to keep any leftover foods; they have paid for all the portions, so it is technically theirs.
7. Have a wet weather plan agreed upon.
8. Be friendly and give good customer service.
9. Look smart and professional at all times.
10. You're on show, so keep your standards high for food and personal hygiene.

ESSENTIAL CONTENTS OF AN EVENT CONTRACT

There is a range of areas that need to be detailed in a contract to create a successful event. These include the number of caterers trading at the event, the food they will be serving, the agreed payment terms, the fees and where exactly the pitch will be situated.

CHAPTER 10

Preparing for a Trading Event

In this chapter, we look at how preparation can be carried out in a well-organised way. This includes the build-up to the event and also what can be done on the actual day. The basic tasks to be completed for a typical working day are described and what to consider when closing down, along with the importance of using lists to stay organised. I have followed this up by giving examples of the considerations to make when setting up your working environment and how this needs to be done to suit your business concept. At the end of this chapter, I have shown things to look at when working in compact kitchens and a diagram of a possible street food unit set-up.

Example Preparation for a Trading Event

There are many considerations to make when you are working up to a busy trading day. The preparation for a trading day can start a week before, and the food can start being prepared a few days before as long as the foods are kept well packaged.

EXAMPLE PREPARATION FOR A BUSY TRADING EVENT DAY

Among the preparations that need to be completed leading up to an event are the ordering of all the ingredients to be used which are not on hand. Food preparation needs to be completed, and all-important documents should be up to date and ready to go, including gas certificates and health and hygiene documents.

THE FOOD TIMELINE PREPARATION: COOKING AND SERVING

I am going to use the Tasty-Burger concept as an example for food preparation, assuming we will be serving food on a one-day Saturday event. First, we need to have our menu completed and ready to go. For example, on our menu we have the Angry Dog Burger and the Casual Tasty Burger with dips. We have a choice of two burgers, and the only difference is that the Angry Dog has extra mustard inside the burger; it's catchy and appealing to customers, yet easily done. Our dips are a homemade garlic mayo and Heinz tomato ketchup, along with the mustard that will also be used for the Angry Dog Burgers.

EXAMPLE PREPARATION LIST

- Make burgers
- Cut tomatoes
- Cut onions
- Make garlic mayonnaise
- Prepare salad – baby gem
- Sauces into squeeze bottles

The tasks can be scheduled by day and time. It's important to keep everything as simple as possible and have as much prepared as possible leading up to the event day. A great piece of equipment for packaging prepared food is the vacuum packing machine; this machine vacuum seals foods air tight in a specialised plastic bag. Professional kitchens use these to great effect, and, nowadays, there are smaller home-style versions available.

This is my diary for the tasks I will be completing, which will be all done at home after I finish my day job. If you are working as a full-time street food business, one option would be to hire a commercial kitchen. In this way, you could do all the prep on a Friday and use their fridges to hold the food overnight.

WEDNESDAY: 7–9 P.M.
I finalise the menu and place orders for meat and all other ingredients from locally sourced suppliers to arrive early Thursday morning before I go to work.

THURSDAY: 6–10 P.M.
The burger mix is made and all the burgers are shaped and refrigerated. I use a branded mayonnaise and roast fresh garlic, mixing the two together.

FRIDAY: 6–9 P.M.
I wash and de-eye the beef tomatoes; I use beef tomatoes, as one slice will fit in a burger. Slice the red onions and prepare and wash the salad, placing all in the fridge. Slice the burger buns, so they are ready to use. The sauces are put into squeeze bottles and all equipment is packed, checked and ready to go.

SATURDAY
Use a checklist for everything needed, and go through the list carefully. Pack the equipment and food into the van and drive to the location. Check for any traffic issues. There is only minimal prep to be done at the site, only finishing touches when serving the Tasty Burgers. The tomatoes can be sliced at the event, and everything else is ready to start serving attendees at 11 a.m.

It's critical to have as much preparation done as possible before the event day. For example, all my burgers are ready to cook and all my sauces are prebottled for quick service. The tomatoes are being sliced on the day, because they do not hold overnight very well once they have been cut. It is essential to use a checklist when loading all food and equipment and go through it well, ticking each item off the list as it is loaded.

It is a good practice to write lists of the jobs that need to be done before the event day; this includes the food preparation, the set-up checklist and the closedown checklist. A checklist of all the documents and certificates needs to be attended to before and on the event day. This will include the hygiene certificates, gas certificates, fridge temperature controls and the cleaning checklist.

The preparation for an event day will all depend on the style of food you will be serving and the unit the business operates from. Although the more complicated the menu is, the more preparation is needed and the more equipment you will need to cook and serve. The specific equipment your unit will need all depends on the foods you have on your menu; this should be taken into consideration when a menu is being designed.

Basics of a Typical Working Day

A working day for a street food entrepreneur will depend on the location of the food truck and at what type of event/festival it is trading at.

THE DAY BEFORE

Make sure all equipment and supplies are ready to go. You have checked everything you need, so you are ready to go the following day.

CHECKING BUSINESS EMAILS AND GETTING TO THE EVENT

Check your emails and update your social media profile. You will need to arrive at the event with plenty of time to set up; this could mean arriving the day before for large festivals or early in the morning at smaller events. On arrival, you will need to locate a festival steward who will direct you to your pitch. On booking your pitch, you would have received important information on who to contact for directions to the location of your pitch. When arriving at your pitch, keep your business set-up in line with the other operators in your location. To set up your business, you will need to locate the fresh water supply, the power supply that you can plug into and where the wastewater is situated.

At many large events and festivals, you will need to have accommodations. There will usually be a site for you to camp at within a sensible distance of your operation.

Weekend Festivals and events will have opening and closing times. With an event license, you are able to open and close on your own terms. It will be most profitable to be open during the whole day. However, there usually will not be significant business before noon (unless your product is aimed at the breakfast customer), but be prepared for the lunch crowd as the rush typically begins at 11 a.m.

CLOSING DOWN YOUR OPERATION

You will need to follow a closing down procedure when you have finished your day or weekend event. Operations will include the draining of wastewater into an approved drain and putting all your rubbish into dedicated bins. The unit will need to be thoroughly cleaned and all health and safety procedures followed, including checking the fridge temperatures if opening the following day.

The Working Environment

When choosing the set-up of your unit, it is essential that it be laid out with your food offerings and menu in mind. A top tip is to plan your menu first because if you know what food you will be serving, then you will know what equipment you need. By compiling a list of equipment, it is possible to buy a unit that has equipment relevant to the set-up you desire. If you have a fried fish and chip option on your menu, you will need to have fryers to use with the toasted sandwich option, and you will need a toaster. Knowing this before you buy is essential and may save you a lot of money and time. But buying a unit with a fryer is pointless to a grilled sandwich business, as it is not going to be of any value.

The working conditions in your unit are going to be affected by your menu set-up. Some pieces of equipment are a lot more awkward to work with in a compact kitchen during a busy service, and a lot of equipment in use will have an impact on your costs. When comparing operating costs, keep in mind that using LPG gas equipment will have a lower cost than electricity.

There are many hazards when working in a compact kitchen space, including burns, cuts, trips and knife safety. All the risks that could possibly happen need to be analysed in your risk assessment as covered in a previous chapter. Once you have decided that you have all the risks covered, you will need to develop systems to control these potential hazards.

THINGS TO CONSIDER WHEN WORKING IN A BUSY COMPACT KITCHEN:

- Always work safely.
- Always have a first aid kit stocked.
- Have plenty of water and drink plenty of water.
- Do a thorough risk assessment.
- Do not keep foods on the floor.
- Keep the floor space clear of obstacles.
- Keep organised at all times and work clean and tidy.

EXAMPLES OF A STREET FOOD UNIT SET-UP

The example below gives you an idea of how a street food business can be set up for an event. As you can see, it is a compact space for the chef and service people to work in. In this example, the cooking is done at the back of the unit, and the food is served to the customers from the prep area. If a gazebo set-up is being used, the cooking equipment can be moved to the front, in this way the customers will see the food being prepared and enjoy that theatre of operation. There may be extra space under the equipment, such as the LPG hobs that will be on a table, and the prep area will have space underneath for storage.

You can imagine how hot and uncomfortable the working environment can become if all the equipment is being fully used during a busy service time. This may be a factor to consider when deciding if a street food business is right for you.

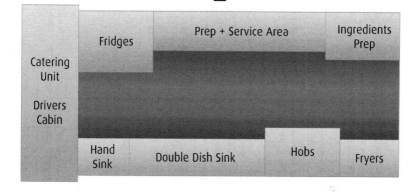

CHAPTER 11

Creating Menus

In this chapter, we are looking at menus for a street food business: how to present them and use correct writing methods. When writing a menu, there are a number of areas that need to be thought about in detail, including how long the foods take to cook and the speed of service. We'll also look at how to test items on the menu including the decoy effect. Finally I'll look at how to cost and price a menu to gain a good gross profit.

What Is a Menu?

A street food business is just like any business in that it needs to make money, gain a good profit and grow. One of the core fundamentals of building success comes from the menu. If a menu is correct, it will sell and make money; if it is wrong, then it will not make good profits and will need to be further revamped *(think of a menu as a sales page)*. A menu is the point from which a customer decides if they want to buy your food or not. Since it is a strong enticement to the customer, a menu needs to be outstanding in its design and descriptions. Always give the correct food descriptions, and be concise with correct spellings and sensible language.

A professional street food business will not advertise food items with odd descriptions, such as 'A nest of fries topped with a trio of sexy saucy dips and warm melted cheese'. All it needs to say is 'Cheesy Chips and Dips'. In attracting and keeping your customers, a good menu is worth its weight in gold. Once they are charmed by your business's atmosphere and by the quality of your foods, it should be enough to get them talking about you and giving you great reviews.

Words such as nestled, drowned, medley, smothered are all often used on menus at fancy restaurants. However, in my experience for a street food business it looks unprofessional and as if the chef is trying to cover up for their lack of experience in the cooking department. A few chefs out there can get away with using these types of phrases; one is Jamie Oliver, who often uses such words as 'awesome' and 'lovely'. But I feel that a menu is best presented so that the food is explained in a comfortable, easy-to-read way, which interests the customer.

Presentation of the Menu

There is a range of ways a street food unit can display their menu; mostly menus will be written in white chalk on a blackboard. The blackboard will either form a part of the unit when the serving hatch is open or an A-board will be used. The writing needs to be clear and concise and to have a short description of each item.

Your description of each menu item is important, and should only say exactly what the food is, without any silly descriptions or strange words, and it should make you feel hungry. It may have a supplier's details on it and the areas where individual quality ingredients are sourced.

Testing Menu Items Presentation on the Board

There is no exact formula on how to write a menu, so different methods can be tested to find the best results. For example, if a menu has five items listed on it, does the order of the items affect the sales? If you find the top spot item sells more, maybe the most expensive item should be placed there.

Use the Decoy Effect

The decoy effect used in many food businesses is a method of using a decoy item to increase sales on more profitable items and to entice the customer to buy more. Study these two menus to see how it works.

Menu A

Cajun Spiced Wedges – £2.00

Angry Dog Burger – £5.50

Cheesy Angry Dog – £6.50

Menu B

Cajun Spiced Wedges – £2.00

Cheesy Angry Dog – £6.50

In this menu, the most profitable item with the highest gross profit is the Cheesy Angry Dog; it is the Angry Dog with a slice of cheese. The profit is a lot higher on the burger with cheese as the price is £1 more; however, the cost is 10p higher, which is a 90% gross profit. The decoy is the 'Angry Dog Burger', so a customer is more likely to buy the most expensive menu item since it is situated beneath burger without the cheese. Perhaps, the customer has a liking for cheese and will give into the temptation to order it.

Chris's Tips and Advice for Writing a Menu

1. Menu needs to be concise and easy to read.
2. Give clear pricing.
3. Avoid silly language.
4. Don't over complicate your concept.
5. Write your menu in English.
6. Give clear description of the main ingredients.
7. Simple menu copywriting is better.
8. If you use a great supplier, list them.
9. Test the order of menu items.
10. Test the pricing and experiment with decoy effects.

A GOOD MENU ITEM DESCRIPTION

The Cheesy Angry Dog Burger
Minced beef burger, brioche bun, beef tomato, baby gem salad, English mustard, cheddar cheese and red onion.

A BAD MENU ITEM DESCRIPTION

The Cheesy Angry Dog Burger
A delicious Cheesy Angry Dog Burger, placed in a toasted brioche bun complemented with a melted slice of mild cheddar cheese, baby gem lettuce, a lovely slice of buffalo tomato, red onion and fiery mustard.

How to Cost and Price Your Menu

There are two main factors to take into consideration when costing your menu: the first are direct costs and the second are your indirect costs. The direct costs are the outlay for all of the ingredients that go towards the menu items, including salt and pepper, oil used in cooking, wastage and the size of individual portions. The indirect costs are all the other expenses that make up the running of the business, such as pitch fees, electricity, cleaning materials and so on.

Wastage

Good waste control is needed to keep costs down. For example, if you are serving a menu with chicken legs and chicken breasts on it and have been buying these separately, it would save money to buy a whole chicken and break it down into portions. By doing this, you will also have wings to use, and soup can be made of the fresh chicken stock.

How to Make a Good Gross Profit

What is gross profit (GP)? It is the monies left after the costs of ingredients have been subtracted from the selling price of the food item. The gross profit percentage is the gross profit set as a percentage.

It's an important concept to understand in order to be successful and grow a street food business. An item on a menu should be priced at the GP% you want to achieve.

Another example to look at:

A pasta dish sells for £6.00 and has an ingredient cost of £2. The profit is £4.00, which is a 67% gross profit.

A steak dish sells for £10 and has an ingredient cost of £6. This has the same profit as the pasta dish at £4.00.

However, the steak dish has a GP% of 40% compared to the pasta's 67% gross profit.

The gross profit is the most important figure to calculate, and items should be priced accordingly.

The Calculation for a GP and a GP% Is Completed in Two Steps

STEP 1
For the GP calculation, subtract the food costs from the selling price of the dish, which in the case of the pasta dish is £6.00 – £2.00 = £4.00.

STEP 2
For the GP% calculation, divide the GP by the selling price and multiply by 100. With this formula, the pasta dish has this GP calculation – £4.00 ÷ £6.00 × 100 = 67%.

All the costs within a street food business need to be tightly controlled, and all direct and indirect costs need to be taken into account to provide the overall net profit to succeed and grow the business. Being financially successful depends on the GP% being consistently adhered to, with a minimal GP% being 70%. It's important to get the best prices on ingredients and to prevent wastage to keep costs down and become successful.

Areas To Consider When Creating Menu Ideas

CHOOSE YOUR FOOD TYPE TO SELL
There are many possibilities for types of food to sell as the list is endless. Some popular foods were listed earlier in this guide, but how do you decide what to sell? You can take inspiration from other street foods from around the world and develop a unique concept around one. Remember, keeping it simple is key, and that you need to maintain a gross profit for financial success. Some other areas to take under consideration are discussed next.

WHAT IS YOUR WHY?
Decide why you want to start a street food business. Is it to change your career, the chance to travel around the country or to make a financially successful multi-vehicle branded business to sell later on? Discovering your why will help you come up with a suitable

business model and will help you decide what foods to sell. Whatever your why, your focus will need to be in a certain area within your street food operation.

WHAT DRIVES YOUR ENTHUSIASM?

To be successful, you will need to keep your enthusiasm levels up, so choosing a concept around foods that you like eating and working with is going to help. When you love the service you are giving, customers and organisers are going to notice, as the authenticity in you and your product will shine through.

WHAT IS THE POTENTIAL GROSS PROFIT?

If you have a plan to grow into a multi-vehicle operation, then you will need to focus on foods and concepts that give the highest profits. The foods will need to be appealing to customers, tasty and have a unique selling point. You will need to conduct a lot of research to get this right from the start; however, you can continuously develop foods with experience gained. Building good relationships with suppliers will help greatly for getting the best prices on ingredients.

IS IT IN YOUR COOKING SKILLS RANGE?

To be able to make a good profit from the street food business, you will need to be able to cook in large quantities. Coming up with foods that are easily produced in volume whilst keeping a consistent quality is going to be a big factor in your choice of dishes for your business. A busy service may see you serving 100 customers in one hour. Can your foods be easily scaled to keep a consistent quality and be cooked in a safe and healthy way.

OTHER CONSIDERATIONS

Work out the costs of food items from your local suppliers, and keep in mind that fish is usually expensive to buy, so the profit margin can be quite low. Foods such as pasta are low on ingredient costs and can be sold at a very good profit margin. There will always be foods that are more popular at events and festivals, such as beef or pork as opposed to a dish built around a food like guinea fowl. A menu needs to be balanced to provide foods that will sell well and yet make a good gross profit whilst being innovative.

CHAPTER 12

Equipment and Food Suppliers

In this chapter, we will be looking at what all street food business need to be aware of. Such as, the equipment that will be needed to run a successful street food business. The equipment that will be specifically needed for each set-up will vary; for example, a set-up serving Tasty Burgers is going to need different equipment than a set-up serving breaded fish and chips. Your menu choice will influence the specific equipment you will need. One piece of speciality kit that I always have when working on events is called the survival kit and it is essential for all set-ups.

The Essential Survival Kit

- Clingfilm – small
- Tin foil – small
- Matches
- Salt and pepper
- Kitchen cloths
- Small chopping board and knife
- Black bin bags
- Clear bin bags
- Spare aprons
- Latex gloves – correct sizes
- Sanitiser diluted in spray bottle
- Dustpan and brush
- Blue paper roll
- Washing-up liquid
- Food temperature probe catering first aid kit

Uniform

Get a few sets of uniforms, which can be a few branded t-shirts and several kitchen aprons. You can have a branded catering fleece for the colder days. In this case, a fleece can be worn with the apron over the top, which is a good idea for a gazebo set-up in the colder evenings.

The Important Health and Safety Documents File and Event Details

All of your documents will need to be filed neatly and organised. These papers should all be ready to go and continuously updated, so you are always prepared for an event. The documents include your food hygiene certificate, food hygiene score certificate, Gas Safety check evidence, PAT test evidence, Public Liability Insurance, risk assessments, cleaning and temperature check lists and your HACCP evidence. All your event details with contact names, numbers, any maps and addresses of the event.

What All Street Food Operators Need to Be Aware of

There are a number of things every unit needs to have to follow health and safety laws. The survival kit has a number of these items, although other essential equipment is needed and are discussed next.

HAND-WASHING SINKS AND ANTI-BACTERIAL SOAP

Good hand-washing practice is extremely important for anybody working with food, as poor hand-washing is a main cause of food poisoning. The Environmental Health Officer will be very strict on having good, well-working, hot water hand-washing equipment. New portable hand-washing sinks can be highly priced, but a starting price of £180 is standard.

ANTI-BACTERIAL SOAP

This is the soap used in conjunction with the PHWS, and it is essential for cleaning hands and preventing food poisoning. You should always have soap available with the PHWS.

HAND TOWELS

Once you have washed your hands, they will need to be dried correctly using disposable paper towels. These towels should always be in supply next to your PHWS and disposed of correctly when used.

SANITISER SPRAYS

The guidelines on sanitising chemicals are very strict, The Food Standards Agency requires all products to meet the British standards – BS EN 1276 or BS EN 13697. This can be found relatively easily at a wholesaler and is the standard that all sanitising chemicals have to meet to disinfect food contact surfaces and equipment. This is important in the control of cross contamination and the spread of E. coli.

DRINKING WATER

Water is essential to a unit, as it has many uses including drinking and cleaning. Check with the organiser to see if there is a main supply of drinking water. You will need a 20-litre jerry can with a tap that can be filled up daily at the site during multi-day events.

COOKING APPLIANCES

Your main cooking equipment will depend on what foods are on the menu. Cooking appliances include fryers, bain-marie, griddles and hobs. These can all be run on LPG gas and using gas is going to keep the costs down, as electricity usage may be high and comes at a higher price.

Another consideration is about your energy source for heat: Will you be operating inside? For inside cooking, electricity may be a better source of heat due to the ventilation requirements of using gas appliances. All gas equipment has to be certified by a qualified gas safe technician.

When cooking foods they should reach a core temperature of 75°C for roughly one minute; this is where your food probe will be used and will have to be sanitised after each use.

PREPARATION OF FOODS

A workspace will be needed for the preparation of foods. A gazebo set-up will need a couple of tables; however, a van/truck or trailer may have all the needed workspace. Folding tables work well and can be broken down, so they will not take up too much space in transport.

Things to remember: when preparing food always use disposable blue roll for cleaning and wiping surfaces not a kitchen cloth. Separate chopping/prep boards must be used for cooked and raw foods to prevent contamination. This regulation needs to be followed when setting up the prep and service areas.

REFRIGERATION

Cold storage of perishable foods is essential, and there are a number of ways to have cold storage. You may have a van/truck or trailer that will have a fridge; if it doesn't, it is advised to buy one. With a gazebo set-up a Thermo Box will be needed, which is a cooler box that insulates the foods and uses a cooling block inside to keep the temperature down to a safe level. Cooler boxes are used to keep perishable foods for longer periods of time on a set trading day. All fridges will need their temperature monitored, as this is part of the required health and safety documents. The correct temperature for fridges is between 1°C and 4°C, and the highest temperature a fridge should reach is 8°C.

HOT HOLDING

Hot holding is another method that can be used. The equipment used may include a bain-marie, which is a metal pot to hold food positioned in a hot water bath that keeps the food hot. The food needs to be kept at a temperature above 63°C and should not be held for over two hours.

BARBECUING

Barbecuing meats is a harder cooking method to control than using griddles, hobs or hot holding. It can be unpredictable and it is critical that the chef is confident and knows exactly what they are doing.

CLEANING

As a legal requirement, all units must have a sink with detergent for cleaning equipment and warm water available instantly. If using a gazebo set-up, a washing-up bowl (instead of a sink) will be needed with hot water available. After the washing-up process, any wastewater will have to drain into a gulley or a container.

POWER SUPPLY

Careful thought is needed when considering the type of power you will be using. Will you be using electricity, batteries or a generator? If you are using electricity, how much will you need for your set-up? Do you just need a minimal amount of power for a fridge and lighting or do you have larger equipment? You will also need the correct extension leads to plug into power from the sites junction box to your unit.

Underestimating the power you will need may result in problems further down the line. Generators may be allowed; however, always check with the organiser and choose a generator carefully. You don't want to buy a generator that is too big to lift or too noisy to work with, and it will need to be put out of the way of the public to shield your customers from the noise and fumes.

FIRE EXTINGUISHERS

Fires are a risk within cooking environments, and you will need to have the correct fire extinguishers for your set-up and a fire blanket. Fire training is included on most one-day health and safety courses.

Other Considerations to Take When Using Equipment

Your food will need to be served in the most cost-effective way possible, and using bio paper products is better than a disposable plastic. Recycling is very important and you need to decide if you will be recycling all of your waste. This means keeping waste food, recyclable materials and non-recyclable materials separate. Any used oils can also be recycled if using a fryer for fish or chips etc. This could also form a part of your unique selling point as people become more environmentally friendly aware.

Be aware of health and safety issues at all times. Extra extension cables, stock or ropes need to be safely tucked away in order to not cause issues with people tripping over them or blocking necessary exit routes in case of emergencies etc. If you need any help in parking your vehicle, use a marshal and follow their instructions, keeping them in sight at all times. During your event, you will be handling a lot of money, so it is recommended to have your cash kept in a safe place to prevent it being stolen.

How to Choose Food Suppliers

In your operation, the supplier is essential to your success as a street food business for giving quality at the best prices. A good and reliable supplier will help you attain your targeted gross profit consistently, and I explained how important this was earlier in the guide.

Once you have decided on the foods that you will be serving and you have created a menu, your next step will be to find good suppliers for your needs. As a street food business, it's essential to use good quality ingredients that will produce a quality product. For example, a customer is more likely to have a good experience with a home-made burger, like the Tasty-Burger concept, which uses quality locally sourced mince beef rather than a frozen bulk burger from a frozen food wholesaler. Choosing a good supplier for your ingredients is an essential part to running a successful street food operation.

A good supplier will deliver the goods on time and at a fair price whilst sticking to your quality control requirements. By choosing a good supplier, great working relationships can be built for your success as a business and the supplier's continued success.

You will need to have a list of requirements that you want your suppliers to meet, and be ready to ask suitable questions around these areas in your selection process.

Your criteria for a supplier to work with can depend on these questions:

- How long does the delivery take from your order being placed?
- Is there a minimum or maximum order for quantities?
- What are the payment terms and conditions?
- Do you use environmental and animal-friendly farming practices?
- Do you run special promotions on products?

By writing down all your requirements before contacting the supplier, you will be well prepared to evaluate the company and their services.

To stock the supplies to your street food set-up, a few different suppliers may be needed. For example, suppliers may only furnish one item, such as a meat supplier, fish supplier, veg supplier or dry goods supplier. As you start your business, it is also an option to visit the producers and pick up the orders yourself and find a whole-saler for your dry goods. MAKRO or BOOKERS are reputable suppliers if they are in your location. Visiting their stores and farms will also give you a better understanding of the products they have available, and it is also a good way to generate menu ideas, too.

How to Find a Local Supplier

There are many quality suppliers out there producing all types of products. Doing an Internet search for your local suppliers is a good starting point or using a local supplier search directory. For example, www.bigbarn.co.uk has many different types of produce and will give information on local suppliers to your area. Another way to source suppliers is by contacting and asking other street food businesses or other food operations in your area, as it is common practice to recommend quality suppliers.

Once you have your suppliers and are using a top-quality supplier with quality ingredients, it is a good idea to mention this on your menu. A simply written list on your menu will show to the customer that you care about the sourcing of your products.

- Check on other street food businesses' websites for their supplier information and who they recommend using.

- Be prepared to negotiate on prices to maximise your gross profit.

- Have a list of all ingredients used in a product, so that you are aware of any possible allergies.

- Keep all your records on file from suppliers including the invoices and any risk assessments that have been taken on delivery.

CHAPTER 13

How to Calculate Your Tender for a Pitch and How Many Portions to Take

This section explains how to calculate a fair price to offer an organiser for a pitch. We look into the considerations you need to make to make a realistic calculation. From the calculations, it is then possible to work out a reasonable amount of portions to cater for, and let's take a look into how this can be calculated. I'll also show the different prices a general purpose unit and a special purpose unit may expect to pay for a pitch at the same event.

How to Calculate Your Tender for a Pitch and How Many Portions to Take

Knowing how many portions you are going to sell is not possible to predict. However, there are measures we can take in our preparation to limit waste and make good profits. There are many factors that will affect your sales, such as your style of unit and the weather, along with how many caterers are on site and what they are serving. Knowing good portion sizes and tendering for a pitches calculation will come with experience at events and festivals, although here are three methods to give you a rough guide.

The first area to consider is that your pitch fee should be 10% to 22% of all of your takings for the event. For example, a one-day event has a pitch fee of £80; therefore, you should be looking to make £800 – £1760. With our Tasty Burger having an average price of £6, the calculation looks like this: £800 ÷ 6 = 133 portions. Using the lower number for anticipated profits is always a good starting point when beginning in the business. If we sell out, then we can up the portion numbers at that type of event. We can also say to reach a 75% GP, we have £1.50 to spend on each burger and can adjust portion sizes and extras to fit this £6.00 selling point.

The second area to consider for a tender offer / pitch fee is the servings per day method. In this example, we calculate how many people we can serve per hour and from this we calculate how many per day. We then multiply the total customers by our calculated average spend. This will give our portion amount and how much to tender. For example, study the following calculation:

An Event Lasting 8 Hours
....

Servings per hour = 40
Total in 8 hours = 320 portions per day
Average spend = £6
Therefore, our tender will be 10% to 22% of 320 x 6 = £1920
Tender = £192–£422

Don't be afraid to negotiate on pitch fees; if it is too much of a financial risk, don't take it. A good opportunity will arise with your preparation and perseverance.

The third area to consider for a tender offer / pitch fee is a longer example calculation, which can be tweaked and changed to suit your own experiences.

This would be for a 12-hour event.

Average percentage of customers who spend money on food at different events:
Music Festivals: 70% to 80%
One-Day Shows: 50%
Local Markets: 55% to 40%

We will follow our average customer buying percentage as above for an event with 3000 attendees at a one-day music festival. We will be selling our Tasty Burger with an average price of £6, using this figure as an average customer spend. We will take 75% of the number of attendees that the organiser quoted to us, which will leave the number of buying attendees at 2250. Now, we have 2250 attendees who may spend £6, resulting in a total event spend of £13500.

This is the point where we have to take into consideration the number of other traders that are at the event and what they are selling. It is also why when the organiser quotes the number of traders and what they sell to us, it should be precise and needs to be written into the contract, as it is so crucially important in our potential earnings calculation.

First, there are certain types of food that are known to sell better than others, such as burgers, so they are known as General Purpose units. Secondly, niche-types of food are known as Special Purpose units, and they are less popular to the mass market.

The organiser has confirmed that there are three General Purpose units and five Special Purpose units. General Purpose units will attract more customers with the figure being around 65%, and they will pay higher pitch fees to do so.

From these figures, we can say that the General Purpose and Special Purpose Unit Sales may be as follows:

General Purpose Units
65% of £13500 = £8775
This will be split between the three General Purpose units = £2925 each.

Special Purpose Units
35% of £13500 = £4725
This will be split between the five Special Purpose units = £945 each.

This example gives the potential earnings from an event, and a tender for a pitch fee can then be calculated by offering 10% to 22% of possible earnings.

A tender average will be £292–£643.

When researching an event to work at, there are a few further calculations that need to be done. From this example, we can see that our Tasty-Burger unit could make £2925. However, can we realistically produce this amount of food in 12 hours? To help us decide, we will calculate potential earnings divided by the average cost of a burger in our example:

£2925 ÷ £6 = 487 burgers sold in 12 hours

This means potential sales could be 40 burgers per hour, which shows we are capable of producing this amount of food and can now calculate how much stock needs ordering etc.

CHAPTER 14

Expanding Your Business and Staffing

In this section, we will be looking at how to expand a street food business and the options available to develop a growing business. The importance of goal setting and having a long-term plan right from the start of your business set-up will be explained. I will also look into the area of staffing: how to know what staff you need and, importantly, how to get them. Finally we'll look at the areas needed to be covered during the interview process of candidates and what red flags to look out for.

Expanding Your Business

Setting goals to reach set timeframes and writing these down will help you to focus on achieving them. Working out where you want to be in five years from your starting point is essential to achieving continued success and business growth. If you have branded your business, and it is easy to set up with appealing recipes and a simple unique selling point, expansion is potentially a fantastic option.

You will not make the real money that's out there until you start to expand and develop your business into a multi-unit operation. Many resources are available to help a business grow successfully, and one of these would be by hiring a business mentor or coach. To achieve your business success faster and better, business training from a mentor, who has been there and done that, is a great investment.

Options for Expanding a Street Food Business Concept

A UNIT UPGRADE

Once you are running successfully and have a good understanding of your brand, operation and useful contacts, you are in a strong position. At this point, you could opt to upgrade your unit to a larger set-up with the possibility of getting into the biggest events, leading to bigger profits and being able to serve more customers and employ more staff.

MULTIPLE UNITS

When you have a great reputation and are doing a good business, customers will be asking about you and spreading a good word about your service. This leads to the possibility of growing your business. You can expand to another unit using the same concepts and branding and manage both units yourself.

CREATE A FRANCHISE

Franchising means you will be able to expand your brand at a fast rate. Your business will need to be fine-tuned and efficient. As a franchisor, you will sell rights to an individual investor for the owner-ship of a unit. You will be paid a franchise fee and receive royalties on the units profit. As the franchisor, you will train the franchisee in the complete running of the business.

POP-UP RESTAURANTS

A pop-up restaurant undertakes the actual restaurant concept. However, it is only open for a set amount of time, which may be one day to several months. The advantage of pop-ups is that you only rent the restaurant for the set period. You can sell tickets to your event, so you will know how many people are booked in. If you have a popular street food unit, it can be adapted to the restaurant-style and be a good way to test the waters of opening a full-time restaurant.

A FULL-TIME RESTAURANT

This is the riskiest option for an expansion, as the costs involved are huge compared to that of a street food set-up. The customers within a restaurant will be different from a street food customer. Testing a restaurant concept in a street food operation first is a good re-search technique rather than going straight into a restaurant.

A FULL-TIME EVENT CATERING OPERATION

Another option for a step-up is similar to a street food business's private hire, where an event caterer will prepare foods in a commer-cial kitchen, and the preparation will be sent out to the event. Event caterers work at weddings, private dinners, canapé receptions, bar-becues etc. and will serve quality food from a range of menus.

Considerations When Assessing the Growth Potential of Your Street Food Business Will Include:

IS YOUR SET-UP EASILY SCALABLE?

When you first start your business, this should be an area that you look into if you want to expand in the future. If you don't consider this in the beginning, you may find you have a successful unit that is very difficult to expand. This is one reason why it is so important to understand your long-term goals and set yourself up to achieve them.

HOW WILL YOU FINANCE YOUR GROWTH?
To expand you will need more cash or capital to use, so make sure your finances can support your expansion? If a loan is needed, will the overall operation cover these extra repayment cost's?

MARKET RESEARCH
Preparation is key and doing your in-depth market research needs to be done to see if there is room in the market for your expansion.

YOUR POSITION DEVELOPMENT
To expand your business, you may need more staff members who are going to need training and further development. Your working role will develop from an owner working and running a single unit to a manager of a whole company.

Essential Information on Staffing
When first starting your street food business, it is unlikely that you will need to hire any staff, especially, if you are working with a partner. Hiring staff will come into play further down the line when you expand your business as your business grows. You may have a long-term plan of acquiring a multi-vehicle operation, and in this case, hiring staff will become very important.

WHAT STAFF DO YOU NEED?
You can only employ the amount of staff that can actually fit in your unit, and this will be your maximum team members. In a standard unit, a maximum of two to three people will be able to work successfully. There are two main types of staff for a street food business: the person cooking and the person serving the foods. These jobs may overlap. Depending on how complicated your menu is will determine how much experience your staff will need, and always a fantastic customer service will be needed.

How to Find Staff

ONLINE
There are many places on the Internet to post jobs, such as gum-tree.co.uk, craigslist.co.uk and indeed.co.uk. Jobs can be posted free on many websites.

WORD OF MOUTH
You may have friends or family who have had experience in the food industry, so ask them if they know anybody who is suitable for a position. Also, a social media posting on your social media can be effective.

Posting a Job Advert
Hiring the right person for any open position is crucial to your business. Placing the correct advert helps bring in the right kind of applicant, and you accomplish this by structuring your advert in a certain way and in listing the experience you want job seekers to have. The layout for a job advert needs to include certain information.

JOB TITLE
Give an eye-catching title for the position that is open.

BUSINESS INFO
Describe the business, working environment and the food you sell.

JOB DESCRIPTION
Describe the responsibilities of the position and the reason for the job availability.

PERSON SPECIFICATIONS
A list of the qualifications and experience the applicant should possess.

HOW TO APPLY
Give a couple of ways for the candidate to send their application, such as by post or by email.

Interviewing Candidates

The interview process is very important, even if a candidate has an outstanding application and CV. It is still crucial to have an interview in order to take a careful look at the candidate. When you are preparing for the interview, you will need to have copies of the candidate's CV /application, the job description, an interview appraisal form and the questions you intend to ask with space to write your notes below the questions.

An interview should begin with questions to help the candidate feel comfortable with the interviewer. Questions need to be written and asked so the interviewee can't just answer with a yes or no answer, but will need to respond with details. Situational interview questions should be written so you can draw out the important information you are looking for, such as the following:

- Tell me about your current role?

- Tell me about a time you have given excellent customer service?

- Tell me about a time you have handled a difficult customer?

Situational interview questions are asked as a way to determine what a candidate will do when faced with a certain situation with the interviewee drawing on a past experience that is similar. During the interview you will be looking for red flags in the candidate's answers, which may be a sign that you do not want to bring them into your business. Red flags may include that they do not have any reliable references, have had a high turnover of jobs in the previous year or have bad personal hygiene.

Towards the end of the interview, ask a few easier questions to help the candidate relax after the tough questions, and find out if they still have an interest in the open position.

There are many areas to cover when employing staff for your street food business, which will need in-depth thought and research. Factors will include contracts of employment, health and safety issues, payroll, workers' rights and so on. All the latest needed up-to-date information can be found at www.gov.uk for all legal rules and regulations when employing a staff.

CHAPTER 15

Knowing if Your Street Food Business Is Succeeding and the Top 10 Tips and Advice

In this chapter, I take a look at the ways it is possible to evaluate the success of your street food business. We look at what key performance indicators are and how to use them correctly. The KPIs we look at include the cost of your foods, your event sales, using your customers' feedback and the importance of being advertised in the media. I follow this by showing you how to deal with complaints and the importance of entering competitions, with the key areas to focus on to win awards. At the end of this chapter, I give my top tips and advice including a look into how to buy and present a vehicle.

Is Your Street Food Business Succeeding?

Whether you are first starting your business or have been running your operation for some time, it is essential to understand if your operation is profitable. This can be found out by completing a set of tasks known as the key performance indicators or KPI. In this chapter, we are going to go through KPIs and how to use them to find out if your business is successful.

Key performance indicators are systems put in place to measure the performance of the different areas of your street food business, and to understand what is improving and what isn't. For example, if your business is being successful, why is it being successful? Learning what is working well will help you concentrate more of your efforts on these successful areas. However, if we discover that there are unsuccessful areas, then corrective measures can be taken immediately.

Key performance indicators are put in place to measure the areas that you have found to be critical to your street food business's success. These can vary from business to business, such as a one-street food operation that may get repeat festival work from an organiser and has high returns, so you may want to analyse the areas at that location. A second operation may work at many different festivals but has more choices on the menu, and you may want to measure which items are selling best and making the most profit. In both of these examples, the key performance indicators are different.

First, we are going to need to make a comprehensive list of all the KPIs that are relevant to your set-up. There are many KPIs that can be measured in a new business and an established one, but here we are going to look at the main KPIs of a street food business.

The main key performance indicators to focus on in your street food business are in the following areas:

THE COST OF YOUR FOODS

I have covered food costs in this guide several times as it is critical to a street food business to get it right and hit the intended targets.

Your total food cost for an event should be no more than 35%, as anything over this will need correcting and improving immediately. Remember we are looking for a gross profit of 75% that means your food costs need to be no more than 25%. This is an essential Key Performance Indicator, which needs to be completely understood to allow for continuous improvement and development.

YOUR EVENT SALES
Your entire event / festival sales data needs to be kept for each and every event. A chart can be made and kept showing all the sales figures from your street food business. You will then be able to see how your sales figures differ; this is especially good for seeing how your business has done year on year. You will be able to analyse your sales figures at a repeat event year on year.

THE HIGHEST & LOWEST SELLING ITEMS
After you have completed an event, all your receipts and stock calculations need to be taken. Make sure that all wastage has been noted down in a wastage analysis document. You will need to count how much of each item on your menu has been sold, as this will give you important figures on your food item sales. Any items that are not selling well can be improved or taken off the menu completely, and other food ideas can be designed around the high-selling food items.

YOUR CUSTOMERS FEEDBACK
Customer's feedback is very important to understand in where to improve your operation, and keeping your customers happy will result in more returning to your business. Listen to your customers comments and encourage them to visit your website and social media profiles, and to leave reviews on sites such as TripAdvisor. A good tip is to set up a lead-capturing system on your website where people can leave reviews of their experience with your business in return for their email, which will help you to build a customer base.

When receiving feedback from your customers, it is advised to reply to their reviews within 24 hours with a thank you. Always keep a check on your reviews and take action on any patterns that you see from the customers. For example, a couple of comments may say that your service was unfriendly during a busy period. From these comments, you will know where to improve your service, which you may have never noticed until it was mentioned. Great customer service is always an essential part to a successful street food business.

YOUR BUSINESS MARKETING FIGURES
If you're just starting out, then it's good advice to leverage free marketing. This means having a website, social media profiles and a YouTube channel, which can all be set up cheaply if doing so on your own. In my opinion, the Internet is a great resource to use for any business. You will be able to analyse which areas you are getting the most interaction with and be able to focus more effort on them. Perhaps, you have a Google+ account and a Facebook page. One of these accounts may get more interactions with people, so it's recommended to focus your time on that one.

It is possible to find which areas are generating conversions the best. For example, your business may have a private hire service that is doing well. How are the customers finding your business and which area of marketing is converting the best? This could be your website's SEO or a Facebook page for example. Once you have a detailed analysis of where conversions are coming from, you can give a greater push to this area of marketing.

YOUR CONVERSION RATE
The conversion rate means how many customers came to your business and how many bought from you. For example, how many visitors came to your website page on a private hire service and converted into a customer? If 100 people came to your page and one converted, then this is a conversion rate of 1%. If you have spent £100 on Internet advertising to get a sale of £1000, this could be an area to focus on. Understanding why they converted will also help you to develop the system.

BEING ADVERTISED IN THE MEDIA
Once you have been seen in the media, analyse how this has affected your sales figures. Have they improved? For example, if your

street food business has a permanent pitch during the week, has the number of customers improved after a mention in the local paper about winning a local competition?

Now you have the key performance indicators that you want to focus on. How are you going to use them? We need to come to a conclusion as to which KPIs are going to add value to your operation, and then focus on improving and growing these specific areas. For instance, we contacted several local charities and offered a free lunch for people in need at this charity and gave a basic cooking lesson to the residents. In doing this, we had a mention in the local media, which resulted in being contacted for several private hire events with high gross profits after people had seen our business in the paper.

In this case, we have gained work from offering our services to a charity for free and giving value. We don't want to just say, 'Get more charity work', as we need to analyse the figures and see where to concentrate our efforts. Think about the answers to the following questions: Which charities are in my local area? How many charities respond to our offerings? Which charities have good connections to the local media?

We know that from our coverage in the local paper that we are receiving more private hire work. Once we understand how many charities are local and what type we need to contact to gain more media coverage, we can then focus on them. We can also measure how many conversions we are getting from different areas of the media, such as newspapers, magazines or radio stations, and which give the highest conversion rates. And then which charities have connections to these specific areas of the media.

Another way of getting a good amount of media coverage is by entering and doing well in competitions. Winners are usually mentioned on the competitions' websites and usually gain media coverage in local newspapers and magazines or even national coverage in the bigger competitions.

HOW TO HANDLE COMPLAINTS

If a customer has visited or is at your street food business and has made a complaint about your food, it is important to resolve the problem as quickly as possible. Take their comments on board and rectify the mistake to turn them into a happy satisfied customer. It is not advised to become defensive about your food, as this reflects very bad customer service. If a complaint has been made several times about a certain item, this should raise a red flag. After receiving a complaint, you could get an opinion from somebody else; ask him or her to try your product and listen to his or her feedback.

The Importance of Entering and Winning Awards

It doesn't matter how big or small your street food business is, there are opportunities out there for you to start winning awards. Awards are going to give your business valuable publicity and recognition as a street food entrepreneur. Awards will look fantastic on your website and will give you instant credibility. Being aware that there are competitions out there you can be entering is important, and also the fact that you could be winning them no matter how small you are is another.

You may not be successful on your first attempt in a competition; however, with perseverance and preparation, I believe success is possible. You should be eager to win awards for your business, but also understand that it takes preparation and experience to gain success.

As a street food business, you have the opportunity to win street food awards. However, remember that there are other awards out there, including small business and start-up awards. There is no harm in entering as many competitions that are relevant to your business as you can.

An important area to focus on is entering the right competitions. If you don't, you will have no chance at all of winning an award.

You may also need to have a minimum of at least one year's trading with financial records. You may need to demonstrate that your business model works and is innovative, and that your business is simply not just a good idea – so be patient and gain some evidence.

Having an interesting story behind your concept appeals to the media, and it gives a journalist something to write about. This could mean you have overcome difficult issues to get to where you are, or you have a really unique selling point. However, you don't want to explain your whole life story to the judges, so just keep it relevant to your business.

Explain to the judges your 'big idea' for your future plans to become even more successful in the future. Let them know that you are just at the beginning of your road to success as you explain your goals. The prizes in many small business awards will come with cash prizes, private mentoring and other benefits to help develop a business. Judges will be looking for a business that will benefit from these prizes, and one that has an exciting solid idea.

There are specific areas to look at when you are considering entering into an award: Check the previous winners to see if they are similar to your business, analyse the award organisers target audience, and find out who will be running and judging the awards. These areas need to be relevant to your own street food business's concepts.

There will be competitions run both locally and nationally. Some of the biggest national street food competitions are listed below.

THE BRITISH STREET FOOD AWARDS

The British street food awards competition is a national competition and without a doubt one of the top competitions in the UK. The competition attracts many thousands of guests who pay for signature dishes on offer by the traders at the final awards in London. The traders go through a regional selection process, with the winners of the regional competition going through to the final.

THE VIRGIN FOODPRENEUR FESTIVAL

This competition is for Foodpreneur's and is run by Sir Richard Branson's Virgin StartUp organisation. The street food business Not Dogs, with their vegetarian hot dogs concept, recently won the tastiest start-up award category. www.notdogs.co.uk.

These are two outstanding national competitions run in the UK for a street food business to consider entering. It is highly recommended to do so as winning this type of competition will give your business massive and instant recognition and credibility. There are also regional competitions for street food entrepreneurs, which are run by local magazines, papers and websites.

Insider Tips & Advice for a Street Food Business

The most important things to remember when running your street food business are to give great value to the customers and offer great quality food that has been tested and refined to give consistently good results. Also, be polite and friendly and give excellent customer service. When you have designed your unique concept, talk to the organisers to build great working relationships, and work with the organiser to create value for the attendees.

Building relationships with the organisers is going to help in gaining the best pitches and keeping them once you have them. When you are creating your USP, visit other street food businesses and take notes on how they operate and how you can improve upon this in your operation.

The Top 10 Tips & Advice

- Find the best events that suit you through research and as you gain experience.
- The industry standard for vegetarians accounts for about 10% of sales.
- Do in-depth research for events to help portion control and tendering.
- Consider the pros and cons of using a commercial kitchen unit.
- Come up with your USP and stick to it through development.
- When starting out, make sure you have enough capital for the first year.
- Know your GP and stick to it through careful sourcing and pricing.
- Always get opinions from others and consider their feedback.
- Keep your cash very safe, which is crucial at multi-day events and weekend festivals.
- Display prices at all times and keep them consistent at events.
- Pay attention to your personal hygiene, such as washing hands and using clean aprons.

Tips and Advice on How to Buy and Present a Vehicle

When you are selecting your unit, there are essential points to remember that will save you money and time in the long run. Decide on your menu first, and then when it comes to buying a vehicle you can select one that already has the equipment you will need. Make sure the vehicle is health and safety passable with a LPG certificate and Electrical certificate. Try to keep your costs down when first starting out.

Once you have a vehicle selected, get it branded by a sign-making design company or completely wrapped in your design to your specific instructions. The set-up needs to be themed and attractive to both the organiser and the customers.

Remember:

- Make sure your unit is clean inside and out.
- Make sure your unit has clean signage.
- Make sure your unit has a clear menu with prices.
- Get a personal hygiene certificate and a certificate display in your unit.
- Register your company and register for self-assessment.
- Get an accountant.
- Offer a unique idea / concept.
- Be aware of new events or people selling pitches.
- Do in-depth research and get evidence and contracts.
- Make sure you have relevant insurance.

UK Street Food Opportunities

There are many events and festivals within the UK over the course of a year. The busy season will be all the weekends in May through September. Points to remember: It is always possible to have rain and this may have a negative effect on attendance figures and sales. It is also possible for events to be cancelled due to bad weather conditions, so always check with the organiser that the event is running as planned.

HOLIDAYS AND IMPORTANT DATES

Jan 1 New Year's Day	**May 2** Bank Holiday
Jan 25 Burns' Night	**May 30** Bank Holidays
Feb 8 Chinese New Year	**Jun 19** Father's Day
Feb 9 Shrove Tuesday	**Jun 21** Summer solstice
Feb 14 Valentine's Day	**Oct 31** Halloween
Mar 1 St David's Day	**Nov 5** Bonfire night
Mar 6 Mother's Day	**Nov 11** Remembrance
Mar 17 St Patrick's Day	**Nov 30** St Andrew's Day
Mar 25–27 Easter	**Dec 25** Christmas
Apr 1 April Fools' Day	**Dec 26** Boxing Day
Apr 23 St George's Day	**Dec 31** New Year's Eve

OTHER DATES

Apr is also known as William Shakespeare's birthday; events will take place to honour the playwright – and 2016 will be the 400th anniversary of his death.

Aug Edinburgh Festival Fringe.

Jun Wimbledon Tennis Championships.

Mar Holi Day.

May Beltane – Beltane (or Beltain) is the Celtic festival of fire.

Jun The Queen's Official Birthday.

Jul Eisteddfod – one of Europe's oldest cultural festivals.

Aug Notting Hill Carnival – Europe's biggest street festival.

Sep London Fashion Week.

CHAPTER 16

Useful Links & Resources

Vital Contact Details for UK Events, Shows & Fairs

Classic Car Shows	www.classicshows.org
Apple Tree Exhibitions and Shows	www.appletree-exhibitions.co.uk
All About Dogs	www.allaboutdogsshow.co.uk
Aztec Events	www.aztecevents.co.uk
Bath And West Showground	www.bathandwest.com
Classic British Festivals and Events	www.classicfestivals.co.uk
The Great Yorkshire Show	www.greatyorkshireshow.co.uk
The Kent Showground	www.kentshowground.co.uk
The Lincolnshire Showground	www.lincolnshireshowground.co.uk
The Royal Norfolk Show	www.royalnorfolkshow.rnaa.org.uk
Staffordshire Country Showground	www.staffscountyshowground.co.uk
Three Counties Showground	www.threecounties.co.uk
Truck Fests UK	www.truckfest.co.uk
Living Heritage Events	www.livingheritagetraders.co.uk
Promoter Of UK Country Fairs And Shows	www.oakleighfairs.co.uk
Santa Pod Raceway	www.santapod.co.uk
Town And Country Markets	www.townandcountrymarkets.co.uk

Vital Contact Details for UK Events & Festivals

WITH ATTENDEES OF 100,000 PLUS:

London Boat Show – Details of London and Southampton Boat Shows	www.londonboatshow.com
Crufts Dog Show	www.crufts.org.uk
The Cheltenham Festival	www.cheltenham.thejockeyclub.co.uk
The Llandudno Victorian Extravaganza	www.victorian-extravaganza.com
The Hay Festival	www.hayfestival.com
Devon County Show	www.devoncountyshow.co.uk
Royal Bath and West Show	www.bathandwest.com
The Royal Cornwall Show	www.royalcornwallshow.org
Glastonbury Music Festival	www.glastonburyfestivals.co.uk
Goodwood Festival of Speed	www.grrc.goodwood.com
International Musical Festival – Llangollen	www.international-eisteddfod.co.uk
Festival Bristol	www.bristolharbourfestival.co.uk
Brockwell Park	www.lambethcountryshow.co.uk
Festival Folkestone	www.warandpeacerevival.com
Festival Warwickshire (Gives demographics on site attendees, average spend and age)	www.thegamefair.org
Festival Brighton	www.brighton-pride.org
Festival Bristol	www.bristolballoonfiesta.co.uk
Cowes Sailing Festival	www.aamcowesweek.co.uk
Falmouth Sailing Festival	www.falmouthweek.co.uk
Festival Hampshire	www.boomtownfair.co.uk

Festival Plymouth	www.britishfireworks.co.uk
Festival Dartmouth	www.dartmouthregatta.co.uk
Festival Lancashire	www.burghley-horse.co.uk
Festival York	www.yorkfoodfestival.com
Festival Bridgwater	www.bridgwatercarnival.org.uk

EVENT DIRECTORIES

Showman's Directory	www.showmans-directory.co.uk
The Outdoor Events Directory	www.outdooreventsdirectory.co.uk
Carnivals UK	www.carnivalarts.org.uk
Event Management Company for Pitches	www.hughmark.co.uk
Air Shows UK	www.military-airshows.co.uk
Christmas Events UK	www.christmasmarkets.com

How To Find Local UK Events: The Pitch Finder Method

THE GOOGLE SEARCH METHOD

To find specific places to trade in your local area this Google search method works well.

STEP 1: Add your selected dates into Google followed by

'Festival Trading Pitch' or 'Event Trading Pitch'.

STEP 2: Follow this with UK or a specific area/location.

Example Google Search

- 18–19 June 'Event Trading Pitch' Cotswolds
- 10–11 August 'Festival Trading Pitch' UK

Useful Contacts For A UK Street Food Business

NEW, USED AND HIRE FOR TRAILERS, TRUCKS / VANS AND GAZEBOS

Jiffy Catering – AJC Catering Trailers	www.cateringtrucks.co.uk
A&R Catering Trailers	www.arwilliscateringtrailers.co.uk
Tow Ability – Mobile Catering	www.towability.com
Tudor Trailers and Equipment	www.tudortrailers.co.uk
Catering Classifieds	www.cateringclassifieds.com
Cater Pods	www.caterpods.com
KK Catering	www.kkcatering.co.uk
Wheelie Box	www.wheeliebox.co.uk
Catering – Trailer-Hire	www.catering-trailer-hire.co.uk
Gumtree	www.gumtree.co.uk
E-bay	www.ebay.co.uk
Custom Designed Gazebo	www.gazeboshop.co.uk

SPECIALISED VEHICLE WRAPPING COMPANIES

It's a Wrap	www.itsawrapuk.com
Boss Dog	www.bossdog.co.uk
Vinyl Revolution	www.vinylrevolution.co.uk

MOBILE CATERING INSURANCE

Mobilers	www.mobilers.co.uk

CASH AND CARRY WHOLESALERS

Bookers	www.booker.co.uk
Makro	www.makro.co.uk

EQUIPMENT

Calor Gas	www.calor.co.uk
Jerry Cans	www.jerrycans.co.uk
Nisbetts	www.nisbetts.co.uk
Homebase	www.homebase.co.uk

STREET FOOD COLLECTIVES UK

Feast on the Street	www.feastonthestreet.co.uk
Food Hawkers – Independent Food Traders	www.foodhawkers.co.uk
Beats Street Food	www.bristoleats.co.uk
British Street Food	www.britishstreetfood.co.uk
Kerb Food	www.kerbfood.com

STREET FOOD TRENDS

The Food People	www.thefoodpeople.co.uk
Street Food	www.streetfood.org.uk
Scoff Street Food	www.scoffstreetfood.co.uk

UK FOOD FESTIVAL FINDER

Food Festival Finder	www.foodfestivalfinder.co.uk

VAN/TRUCK/TRAILER NEWS AND REGULATIONS

Commercial Fleet	www.commercialfleet.org

ENVIRONMENTAL PACKAGING

Packaging Environmental	www.packagingenvironmental.co.uk
Biopac	www.biopac.co.uk

GROSS PROFIT CALCULATOR

Gross Profit Calculator	www.grossprofitcalculator.com

VITAL INDUSTRY CONTACTS

Nationwide Caterers Association	www.ncass.org.uk
Health and Safety Executive	www.hse.gov.uk
Food Standards Agency	www.food.gov.uk
NICEIC (electricians)	www.niceic.com
Gas Safe (licensed gas fitters)	www.gassaferegister.co.uk

CATERING EQUIPMENT AUCTIONS

W&H Peacock	www.peacockauction.co.uk
Catersell	www.catersell.co.uk

LPG COOKING APPLIANCES

Catering Suppliers	www.catering-equipment-suppliers.co.uk

STREET FOOD COMPETITIONS

NOEA	www.noea.org.uk
Café Life	www.thecafelife.co.uk
British Street Food	www.britishstreetfood.co.uk
Virgin StartUp Foodpreneur	www.virginstartup.org

VEHICLE SIGN MAKER – DESIGN COMPANIES

Sign Express	www.signsexpress.co.uk
Display Sign	www.displaysigns.net

TO ACHIEVE A GUARANTEED FIVE STAR FOOD RATING

The Food Safety Guru	www.foodsafetyguru.co.uk

For Important Health & Hygiene Downloadable Documents Search for: *Safer food, better business for caterers.*

Conclusion

By reaching the end of this guide, you have gained the business knowledge to start following your career as a street food entrepreneur. Now is a fantastic time to enter the fast developing, exciting and challenging career as a street food entrepreneur. Whether you are an experienced chef or just want to become a food entrepreneur, there is an opportunity right now for you. The successful people who break into the industry as a street food entrepreneur will have four similar qualities in common: self-belief, fully prepared, self-motivated and persistent.

There is a lot more support for people wanting to operate their own street food business in 2016 than previously, and this will most likely be the trend as interest continues to grow. When deciding on your type of street food business, it is recommended to do in-depth research, read a lot of books and gain experience. Think about what you are doing within your business and do not rush your decisions; however, make sure action is taken.

When starting out, be prepared to learn a lot, work hard and be dedicated to succeeding in your street food business. Overall you will need to have a good attitude to thrive, and if a situation becomes too comfortable, put yourself out there and look into the bigger events and festivals.

Thank you for taking the time to read this book, and THANK YOU again for your interest. I have greatly enjoyed writing this book, and I hope my guide will help you achieve your goals as a street food entrepreneur. Good Luck!

Most Importantly Enjoy Yourself and Give Value

A Few Final Thoughts

You have now reached the end of this street food business guide. And, hopefully, you are now well prepared to advance your career into a street food operation. Before you start putting all you have learnt into practice, I have a few final pieces of advice.

There are many opportunities out there to start and grow your business, at excellent events, markets and festivals. The people who gain the best opportunities out there will be the ones who are well prepared and have a belief in themselves that they will succeed no matter what anybody tells them. The key components to start, run and grow your street food business are listed below:

1. SELF-BELIEF
Regardless of what anybody tells you, you can move your career forward. Be confident and believe in yourself, and if you have weak areas, then improve upon these.

2. BEING FULLY PREPARED
Prepare for everything, this is the key to your success. Good preparation will improve your performance and generate great results. As the saying goes – fail to prepare, prepare to fail. Well, prepare to succeed! Using this guide you can gain all of the personal skills you need to make a success of yourself in the industry.

3.SELF-MOTIVATION AND PERSEVERANCE
How much do you want to succeed as a street food entrepreneur? It is extremely important to keep your motivation levels up. When you make mistakes, learn from them to perform better the next time. You should always be looking to improve on everything that you do. Perseverance is the key to achieving success. With hard work and discipline, you can become anything that you want to be. Thank you for reading; I wish you all the best of luck.

Books By This Publisher

- How To Become A Chef
- Starting And Running A Street Food Business UK
- Commis Chef Interview Questions & Answers
- How To Bake A Cake

Contact Details

Website Addresses and Courses
BAChefUK
www.becomingachef.co.uk

Cake Baking Courses
www.bakeacakecourses.com

Street Food Business Course
www.streetfoodbusinesscourse.com

You Tube Channels
BAChefUK

Social Media

Twitter   -   @BAchefUK

Facebook   -   BAChefUK

Pinterest   -   BAChefUK

Instagram -   BAChefUK

Disclaimer and Copyright